OCCAM'S RACQUET

OCCAM'S RACQUET

12 SIMPLE IDEAS FOR SMARTER TENNIS

Marcus Paul Cootsona

PRO TENNIS PRESS
Menlo Park, California

OCCAM'S RACQUET
12 Simple Ideas For Smarter Tennis by Marcus Cootsona.

PRO TENNIS PRESS
P.O. Box 1296
Menlo Park, CA 94026, USA

To book Marcus Cootsona for a speaking engagement, visit www. Protennispress.com.

First Edition.

Library of Congress Cataloging-in-Publication Data has been applied for.

ISBN: 0615513816
ISBN-13: 9780615513812

To Stanley W. Sexton.

CONTENTS

A DUDE AWAKENING

(The Pre-Game Talk)

"It hardly does much good to have a complex mind without actually being a philosopher."

Saul Bellow, *Herzog*

If you play tennis, you want to play better tennis. That is the nature of the sport. You may have started playing tennis for a variety of other reasons, but the idea of limitless improvement is one of the things that keep you competing and practicing. If you're like most players, you believe that your best tennis is still ahead of you; not as some abstract ideal, but as a real, palpable and attainable goal. Like washboard abs, an Aston Martin or a nap once a week.

In order to reach this goal, you want to take every step possible. You take lessons from an enthusiastic young teaching pro. You watch tennis on your big screen HD TV; maybe play in a league or in tournaments. You spend your hard-earned money on books like this one. You even buy some copies of your new favorite read for close friends and then blog it, tweet it and friend it. You do everything you can to improve; short of actually quitting your job, living out of your car and playing full-time. But even with lots of hard work, dedication and cash outlays, you may still find that there are big pieces of the game that seem to elude you. Not just where to stand on the seventh point of a tiebreaker either. In some cases, you may just *sense* what those pieces are, but you can't quite pin them down.

Your instructor, a Mr. I.M. Headstrong, is teaching you the "pro game", but it doesn't always make sense. It doesn't always work either. Sometimes you wonder about his effectiveness *and* his silly name. Feeling that there's something wrong with *you*, you work even harder, but progress still comes slowly. You're giving it your all but you just seem to be stuck, idling in one tennis gear. The improved tennis you've envisioned for your future doesn't seem to be getting any closer. But thanks to all the workouts, your abs are ripped, you're rested and fit and you sure look good in that Aston Martin – T-Shirt.

APPROPRIATE READING MATERIAL

Is this book for you? Well, if you are a beginning, intermediate or advanced player who wants to escape sports participation neutral and put their tennis game back in a forward gear, it is. If, on the other hand, you want to work really hard and tread water until the dawn of the next Millennium, then no. You see, great tennis, especially great match tennis is not just about strokes. It's about nice clothes, shiny, aggressively decorated racquets and maybe a slight tan. And more than that, significant, sustained progress in the game of tennis comes from learning how to use your *head* to help your body wring the most out of your ability and time and goals on the tennis court. **In order to fulfill that lofty theory and rhetoric, we are going to examine the mental side of the physical game and the physical side of the mental game and most importantly how those two sides work together to produce better *match tennis*.**

This book is for players who want to improve their *approach to the game* and be successful on the court more often. That may mean hitting more consistent, powerful shots. It may mean erasing self-doubt and distraction during matches. It may mean winning more. But it absolutely means playing a more effective, thoughtful, deliberate game. This book contains no shortcuts – there are none in tennis. (What, no "Win at tournament tennis in two days?") But it contains no long-cuts either. Long-cuts are paths that create years of great effort and mental agitation with achingly slow progress. (Think: high school history class.) This book is dedicated to the twin ideas of hard work and smart work, both mentally and physically. More accurately, that's a total of four ideas, but then again, this is a tennis book, not a math book.

To quote the English philosopher and statesman, Francis Bacon (as all tennis books should), "Reality to be commanded, must be obeyed." In the same way, so must the tennis court (and for that matter, the tennis brain) be obeyed to be commanded. This book presents a new way to *think* about tennis – a way to command it by obeying it. This book is not about quick fixes. And it is not about the thoughtless, inappropriate instruction, critiques and commentaries that have fixed the idea in many tennis players' heads that they are hopelessly square and outdated if they don't hit like the pros they see on TV. Square and outdated often wins matches. The nerdy dude in the 4" inseam constructed shorts, playing a Head Graphite Edge with Bluestar strings and flat strokes often takes apart the open-stance, over-spun groundies of the "pro game" devotee in the Nadal sleeveless. Whichever of these (or other less extreme) characterizations describes you, **this is a book filled with ideas and techniques you can start using right now to improve your strokes and your mental approach to the game.** This is a book that will reintroduce some sense and proportion and simplicity back into your playing. It will help you to find reasons for *what* you're practicing and *how* you're practicing it. *A way to use your brain to win more sets and matches.*

IDENTITY HEFT

So who am I to be making these claims? What qualifies me to help you? Here's the short version. I played junior tennis, high school tennis and stopped playing competitive tennis in college. I found that I loved instructing more than competing. I have no professional tennis playing pedigree, and can make no claim to expertise based on an illustrious playing career. I have, however, been gainfully employed as an instructor for the past 29 years and my students have succeeded at every competitive level and still talk to me. Since I was a player for whom tennis skills came only with a great deal of toil and effort (translation: I was a mediocre athlete), I believe I also understand what the average player is up against trying to learn this game.

I know also that the best instruction I received was step-by-step (modular, is maybe a better, or at least more pseudo-scientific-sounding term) and conducted on a need-to-know basis. My instructor and I would work on one pointer, learn it and move on to the next one. That way of working stuck to me like the Spandex tights under the original Agassi jean shorts: to this day, I'm a pitiful multi-tasker. My best instructors never mentioned *their* playing results (although later I learned that some of them were more than a little impressive), instead they were interested in *my* results. They wanted to help me follow the most direct path to a great game. They cared only about progress, not about criticism. As my wife Melinda (a fine instructor in her own right) once said, "There are many critics, but very few teachers." I've met the critics and was lucky enough to have been taught by one of the teachers.

CHARDONNAYS AND STRATEGY

What has always stitched all of the parts of my crazy quilt tennis life together is a central belief that tennis is a game worthy of serious consideration, sober study, inspired playing and the occasional philosophic detour. Though I have devoted myself to this sport, I had never thought of writing a tennis book. That is, not until one recent August 10th. That was the day I saw the consequences of players under the influence of unfocused strategizing, too much input and in some cases too many kick-off party chardonnays. Watching them spun me in a new direction.

On that day, my son and I set up an outdoor tennis specialty booth at an adult league playoff tournament. We had an excellent opportunity to listen to the players and their coaches discuss their strategies and stroke ideas for their upcoming matches. This was an all-day, ear-opening experience.

That evening at dinner, talking over what we had overheard, we agreed on one big idea. Tennis is *not* a natural team sport; everyone becomes a de facto coach. The amount of complex tactics, measures, counter-measures, pairings and line-up strategies the players on these teams were considering and suggesting to one another was vast and, in fact, was only limited by the amount of time available between matches. And yet, in watching the matches that day, only a few of the numerous, complicated strategies could be used or made effective. Why? Two reasons. One, these players had not taken into account some fundamental ideas that affect everything that happens on the court; and two, no one could keep that volume of detail in their head and still play tennis.

As we discussed their approach to the matches and their own games, I realized that I wished I could talk to these players and help them to play *simpler*, *smarter* tennis. What was missing from their arsenals was one fundamental idea – *they all needed to hit the ball into the court more often*. Call me wild-eyed reformer, but that is what it boiled down to. They needed to obey the boundaries of the court to command them.

They didn't need to think *more* about what shots to hit and what strategy to use. Instead, they needed to think more *carefully* about what would actually help them win their matches. These players were all using their brains a lot. In fact, most of them were overusing their brains to try to win their matches. They were all dedicated to improving. But unfortunately, they didn't have the right kind of knowledge and, in some cases, they didn't have the right kind of strokes. They were thinking *hard*, but they weren't thinking *smart*.

OCCAM'S RACQUET

Tennis is a game of boundaries; a game played between sets of perpendicular and parallel lines. A game in which it is easily possible to become too enamored of the racquet's power or too beguiled by the court's enticing geometry or too concerned with what your opponent will do when you hit the shot you're planning to hit three shots from now. But before any Byzantine strategies or complex maneuvers can become effective, you first have to conquer the basic fact that no points are scored if the ball doesn't go in. As my coach used to say about the serve: "The only thing the serve *needs* to do is to go into the box." A good coach, like a good player knows how to reduce the imperatives.

Hit the ball in the court. Simplify the sport to its essence. The more I thought about this concept, the more I (naturally) began to think of William of Ockam, the medieval philosopher best remembered (to the extent he is remembered) for what has come to be known as "Occam's Razor"; the theory that if a number of explanations describe a situation or solve a problem accurately, the *simplest* explanation is to be preferred. This one meta-philosophical idea provided a basis for many advances in philosophy and helped pave the way for the heliocentric view of the solar system, the scientific revolution and drive-through espresso huts. It's also the basis for this book. We'll call our method *Occam's Racquet*:

taking the simplest true explanation as the best way to play great and enjoyable tennis.

Simple incidentally, doesn't mean *simple-minded*. There's been enough "This, That or The Other Thing for Dummies." And there's been more than enough how-to-hit-the-best-strokes-ever-in-one-lesson sourcebooks. Strokes are best learned *live*. *Concepts* that tell you *why* to hit the strokes you're learning are best taught in books; except that's not what's usually *in* tennis books. This sounds revolutionary, but I am not here to revolutionize tennis instruction. There's been quite enough of that too. Tennis is not a complicated game, but it can be difficult. There's every reason not to re-make it, but to re-take it back to some core ideas that will make it simpler no matter what type of strokes you're learning. In the pages that follow, I will teach you to hit with Occam's Racquet so you can hit better with your own racquet. This reductionist method may change some or much or most of what you're doing and thinking about tennis now. It may change your strokes. It probably will change your strategy. I certainly hope it will change your mind.

ACKNOWLEDGMENTS

First of all, to Melinda Lomax Cootsona, my wonderful and indulgent wife, who reviewed the manuscripts and supplied encouragement, help, copy proofing and joke editing throughout the writing process.

To my son, M.J., who spent many hours watching lessons, playing tennis with students good-naturedly trekking all over Northern California to watch student tournaments and help with our peripatetic retail sales adventures, and for being the best son I could possibly imagine (especially since he actually likes golf better.)

To my parents, Tom and Ruth, for introducing my younger, better-looking self to this great game and allowing me to always pursue it and every other wild idea that came into my head wherever it led me.

To Dr. Peter Klein and Marvina White for taking the time to read the manuscript and offer their thoughts on its worth and various virtues.

To my great friend, Paul Guay, for the many years of three-hour-a-day writing tutorials.

To William of Ockham for his enduring contributions to clear, concise thinking in philosophy and especially tennis.

OCCAM'S RACQUET

To my various tennis teachers, for teaching me what to teach, what not to teach, how to teach and how not to teach. It was all valuable.

To my friends and benefactors, George and Mimi, for allowing me to use your beautiful court for these many years.

To my students, for giving me the opportunity to spend my days with the most interesting, intelligent and engaged group of personalities I can imagine, teaching me how to teach what is important and paying me to learn.

PLAY NOT LIKE THE PROS

(The Warm Up)

"The conventional wisdom is just that: it's conventional. And it may or may not be wisdom."

Anonymous

"Learn to play like a pro." " I teach the 'modern' tennis game, the game you currently see the professionals playing." "Where champions are made." These are some promises made by tennis "academies" in our area. I'm sure that without much searching, similar inflammatory bombast could be culled from many areas of the country; claims used to promise kids and their parents and others with a dream that the heralded teaching method is indeed the one *true* method for incubating a lot of little pros, or at least players who play like little pros, no matter what size they are. Putting aside the question of whether this group teaching style is very effective and more specifically *which* pros are to be emulated, we are left asking even more basic questions: what exactly *is* the "pro game", does everyone *need* to play like a pro and do the banks still write home-equity lines big enough to pay for it?

OCCAM'S RACQUET

GAMING THE SYSTEM

Not only the academies, but also many current instructors are trying to sell a similar strain of instructional indoctrination of a pro-game method; a win-this-way system good for a one-style-fits-all teaching template. Most of these we'll-teach-you-to-play-like-the-pros systems ask students to make extensive, time-consuming changes to their games. A sure way to discombobulate the student, sell a proprietary racquet with a weird string job and guarantee an endless flow of lesson billings. But what about any of the other merits of this approach? Well, you may get treated offhandedly by a gruff former satellite pro, hear tales of their tour exploits and compete with dozens of other players employing the *exact same strokes and tactics you are*. More positively though, everyone at these academies is certainly unfailingly "on message"; there's never a lapse in the orthodoxy.

And that's the thing about a system, once you begin to promote it, it's hard to admit that the student may be better suited for a different approach and may be fine without the system. In an alternate universe, the choice would be to look at the student as an individual and take their innate style and work with it and develop it. However, redefining the student as a singular player with specific requirements would lead to a monumental disruption of the system and academy cash flow. It would also logically suggest that there is, in fact, no one correct, received method for hitting tennis strokes; and that what really matters is what physical abilities, learning style and playing personality the particular student brings to the lesson.

In the January 2010 issue of GOLF magazine, instructor, Peter Kostis, quoted a legendary golf instructor named John Duncan Dunn, who said back in 1931: "An instructor should see how much he can leave alone, not how much he can change, and he will get better results by helping the pupil along his own natural bent." Clearly an outdated view in the tennis universe. Thankfully, Carbon 14 dating gave us the quotations' precise age for archaeological reference and ancient cultures' research and preservation purposes.

CARRY A MEDIEVAL STICK

Occam's Racquet is going to take some swings at the general notion that as the pro game goes, so should the rest of the tennis world go. As a working teaching professional, I am often referred players, adult and junior, who have started playing with, or have had their game altered by instructors using the "system" suggested by the "I will make you a pro" credo. It is the prevalent instructional attitude for most teaching pros, especially those at clubs. It also seems to be the dominant attitude at resorts; where the pro typically has only one day to really mess up your game. The quintessential junior player schooled in this way, by Mr. I.M. Headstrong or one of his allies comes to me with a heavy topspin forehand, an underdeveloped backhand, an unusable serve and no volleys or overheads. (In other words, somewhat less than the complete game.) Similarly, adult players whose functional, traditional games have been re-engineered by their club pro or the enthusiastic resort pro, find their once solid games in stroke and grip change confusion. They are now expending supreme amounts of effort to try to use the new grip and spins they have been convinced to add to their arsenal; as well as clothes that make them self-conscious and rock-hard plastic strings that send tremors through their hitting side forearm.

If I were looking for an annuity, I should send each of these I-will-make-you-a-pro instructors a thank you note and a nice gift – they have given me students whose games will take years to correct. However, I want everyone to play better, smarter tennis and the sight of some of these nice people led into an intricate web of instructional stickiness just makes me want to – write this chapter.

PROPONENTS AND PRO OPPONENTS

Why do I object to this type of game and how does it break Occam's Racquet? Very simply, the type of game these instructors teach is the opposite of a simple, repeatable playing style (I guess that would make it complex and sporadic) – the style that would make match tennis fun and rewarding for most of the tennis playing population. I hesitate to do it, but I'm going to invoke the famous tennis instructor and academy pioneer, Nick Bolletieri, who in a recent *Tennis* Magazine article about the forehand said, "I tell these USPTA (United States Professional Tennis Association) guys that sometimes they just make things too complicated." My friends, if even the guy who jump-started the whole tennis academy gocart sounds an alert like that, we should all pay attention.

The "pro game" as it is being interpreted and disseminated is technically complex, hard to learn and hard to maintain without a high degree of on-court practice. (And it's not always attractive to watch.) In the abstract, it sounds like a sensible and wonderful goal. I mean, who wouldn't want to play the like pros we see on TV? And if teaching professionals aren't trying to take players to this level, who is? No doubt the job of teaching professionals is indeed to develop the most skillful player possible. That and move as little as possible, never bend their knees and compliment students despite the shot they just hit. But for various reasons – many of them having to do with real-life intruding on tennis time, others having to do with the student not needing to gratify Mr. Hitt Mighway's instructor ego – not everyone should learn this more complex version of the game; at least not at the *beginning* of their development.

For humans in the actual physical world to play better, smarter tennis, they *and their instructors* need to always keep in mind these simple questions: What are the player's goals? What is the player's ability? And maybe most important, how much is this player really going to be able to practice? It is not logical, desirable or good, old old-fashioned considerate to saddle a mature adult player who can only practice one to two hours per week with strokes that demand three to four hours *a day* of practice. It makes the teaching pro look tough and demanding and certainly creates a dependent student. But does it produce better tennis players or happier people? Still, it is done all the time; and it is not making those tennis games any simpler or easier. And let's face it, the sport is challenging enough already.

BESPOKE STROKES

Tailor the strokes to the student. If an adult, who doesn't have time for hours of daily practice, begins to learn strokes that have intense practice requirements, how will he or she perfect or even feel comfortable with these strokes? If an adult league player shows up at a resort with a perfectly usable flat forehand, does it make sense for the pro to change their stroke in one day by switching them to a radical new grip for extreme top spin? It does if they want to make their mark and prove that they made a difference. Coloring your hair purple makes a difference too. But it's not for everybody. And is the difference made in that player's strokes worth sending their game into a three-month tailspin?

If a junior who is involved in three other sports comes to the club pro for lessons, but actually only plays for a few months out of the year, does it really make sense to teach him or her heavy top spin strokes and neglect the rest of his or her complete game? It does if you want everyone to know that the young virtuoso netting, fencing and over-spinning the ball is doing so because they're learning *your* method. Which reminds me, I knew an instructor who used to tell his students, *"I'll* tell you when you can say you take lessons from me."* (No player was going to represent *him* before their time.) None of this makes sense to me and yet these are the types of students who come to me for rehabilitation. So what is the alternative? What type of instruction is best for the average player with a restricted playing schedule?

The most effective teaching approach for building a game that can progress to any level, is one that is *modular* and *progressive*; using strokes that are appropriate to the student's abilities, life demands on practice time and of course their goals. I prefer to build a set of skills, one on top of the other as the student progresses. The student learns to do a certain skill well and then adds more nuances to that skill. We might characteristically work in this type of progression: learn to hit a flat, drive forehand first, then move on to slice and then to top spin. In this way, the student not only learns how to hit through the ball before learning to hit spin, but also has a thorough understanding of the need for the strokes they're hitting. Just as importantly, they have a stroke that is usable and functional at each step of their development.

SYSTEMATICALLY UNSYSTEMATIC

Of course, my non-system is also a system. But that's okay, contradiction and ineffability are the time-tested hallmarks of deep truth. This modular stroke-building can progress all the way to the pro level also. If a student (after the obligatory conference Skype with their parents, agent, manager, physical therapist, trainer, investment advisor and me) decides that they want to be a pro, we work on developing sound fundamental strokes that can be added to in order to eventually create pro strokes. If the student progresses that far, great; if not, then that student will still have usable strokes for the rest of their life. The goal of this type of modular instruction is not necessarily to play like a pro, but to play; and play successfully.

I have worked with junior players who have been coached at clubs in this high-maintenance style who hit so much wristy top spin that they can't even start a rally. And when they do manage to put the ball in play, the spin and angle make it unreturnable. Where is the utility in such a stroke? Where is the fun? Where is the self-esteem? Players schooled like this cannot play recreational tennis later in their lives, if (the unthinkable happens and) they don't make it on the pro tour. Players like this can't even experience the simple joy of playing with friends or their parents in a casual game. And contrary to what the 22 year-old teaching pro, a Mr. U.R. Destined, wants us to believe, this is where their games are probably going to end up, no matter what they achieve as juniors.

FUNNEL VISION

Top spin forehands are not the only blind spot in this instructional vision, but they're a big one. Since very few playing pros on tour come to net to volley these days, fewer instructors know how to or even care to teach correct volley technique. One local academy focuses so heavily on groundstrokes, that many of the students have barely developed serves; let alone volleys or overheads. Neglecting net play makes sense to those ensconced in the pro game paradigm; the pros don't use volleys. Well, again, if (god forbid) these academy prodigies don't make the singles team at school or don't get on tour and want to play a recreational game with friends, well then, they're out of luck. Most doubles is still played at the net using volleys. And overheads.

On the applied level, find an instructor who wants to build a complete game, piece by piece and most importantly gives you better reasons than "that's what the pros do" to justify what you're being taught. Or, at least if he/she gives this reason, ask, "which pros?"

Good instruction and good tennis all recognize that your speed of learning, your physical attributes and your interests are unique to you. If they weren't, then everyone could be taught out of the same play-book. (Wait. People are doing that). Develop a game that suits you and doesn't try to make you into a clone of the latest prodigy. I'm not saying don't ever impart top spin, crunch kick serves or hit open stance while leaping about. And I'm certainly not saying don't aspire to great things. What I am saying is consider who your child is and who you are. Not just for tennis either. How much are you really going to practice? Do you need an exotic, high-maintenance stroke if you're only playing an hour a week? Wouldn't it be better to adopt a simpler plan that you could actually maintain, even if you didn't play for six months? Wouldn't you like strokes that would hold up at every age? The modern game has its place for the right player at the right point in their advanced development. But the simple, intelligent game has its place too for players of all ages with less than full-time dedication to the sport.

BOILING WATER

Just as the boundaries of the court must be obeyed to be commanded, so must our own physical abilities and available time be considered if we are to play rewarding, successful tennis. You're certainly welcome to jump into the deep end before learning the crawl; cook Beouf Wellington before boiling water or learn the grace notes without learning the piece of music itself. Just realize that if you proceed heedlessly and take things out of order, you threaten to end up playing arpeggios and trills before you can read music. You also threaten to stretch out the learning curve with whichever instructor you choose.

Okay then, enough griping, dissention and dissection. I think we're done with that. (Although I can't promise that we're *done*, done.) Still, we're not here to bury other instructors, but instead to elevate your game, specifically your match game. What's ahead for us is a program for effective physical and mental matchplay tennis: tennis that can work for *all* players. I have laid out what I consider to be the most important building blocks of the intelligent game for players of all levels. The stroke instruction is general and the psychological advice can be used in tennis, in other sports and in life on-going.

The two major sections of this tomb are broken down into "sets", six chapters ("games") for the physical side and six chapters ("games") for the mental side. They represent the areas that are the most critical to developing useful and lasting match tennis skills; and are the most general ideas I focus on with my students. As you will no doubt notice, the divisions into the physical game and mental game mostly hold, but in some cases the two are necessarily intertwined. All of which proves that the two, while separated arbitrarily for our purposes, are nevertheless two sides of one whole being; the complete player. You.

Some players may find some of the advice too basic while many others may be encountering it for the first time. So, please, you bought the whole book, read it all. There is worthwhile advice for all level players. In fact, read it in whatever order you like. The chapters will make the most sense sequentially, but each one can also stand on its own. Use what you can and file the rest for use later. The pre-game talk is complete, let's serve up our first set.

THE FIRST SET

LET'S GET PHYSICAL

(The Physical Set)

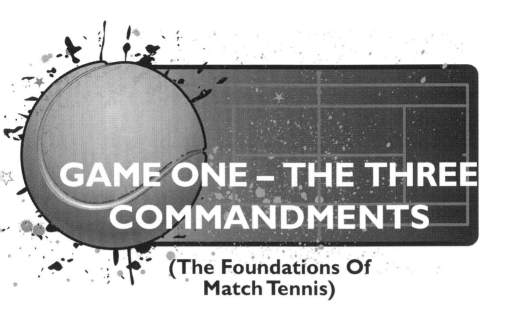

GAME ONE – THE THREE COMMANDMENTS

(The Foundations Of Match Tennis)

"If you have an important point to make, don't try to be subtle or clever. Use a pile driver. Hit the point once. Then come back and hit it again. Then a third time – a tremendous whack."

Winston Churchill

The first step in our march toward simpler, smarter tennis is to reduce match tennis to a small set of fundamental ideas; three basic rules to be exact, re-framed, re-marketed and recast in 21st Century short-attention-span-multi-task-succinct text and tweet worthy contemporary jargon speak as: **The Three Commandments.**

As we know, the test of any good formula (look both ways before you cross, $1+1=2$; $E=MC^2$) is its ability to express big concepts in the fewest possible characters. Unlike Einstein's famous formula, getting the full value out of the three basic rules of match tennis doesn't require complex mathematics or flights of conceptual physics fantasy; just a decent memory, available court time and a moderate attention span.

The three commandments are easy to remember, which I find helpful. And like a ready smile, cultural openness and negotiable currency, they travel well and they are effective in all situations; from a casual match at the courts or the club to the highest reaches of the pro game. Most importantly, like the expressions "system is freedom", "be here now" and "Facta non Verba" (three Latin words), or (more specifically, deeds not words), these simple rules go deeper than their one-sentence formulations suggest. These are the three basic rules for *all* levels of tennis in *all* match situations (I told you the instruction would be general) –

FIRST COMMANDMENT – GET YOUR FIRST SERVE IN
SECOND COMMANDMENT – CLOSE ON THE SHORT BALL
THIRD COMMANDMENT – HIT THE BALL BACK THREE OR MORE TIMES

If you take nothing else from this book, learn the three rules. (Although I hope you can use one or two other ideas.) That's why this is game one. Whatever style strokes you use and whatever your tactics are, these rules will give you a steady set of bearings to successfully navigate the shoals of match competition against any level opponent.

COMMANDMENT #1 – Get Your First Serve In

Forget kick. Forget speed. Forget spin. Forget placement. Until you can get seven out of ten serves over the net and in the service box consistently, you have only one job – *practice until you can.*

The serve is the most important stroke in match tennis. If you always hold (that is, win) your serve, you need only one or two breaks (winning the opponent's serve) to win a set. This makes the tennis arithmetic easy. Pete Sampras used this simple formula to win 14 Grand Slam titles and finish at number one in the world for six consecutive years. Pete rarely won sets 6–0 or 6–1. He didn't need to. And, his statistics suggest, he didn't really care to. He did the math. And the math is persuasive. He often won sets by only one service break. But, like someone inheriting fifty billion dollars, that is all he needed.

This isn't to suggest that you should calibrate your efforts so you win your matches by wispy thin margins. If an opponent can be vanquished 6 – 0, 6 – 0, proceed. But even in a close contest against a well-matched adversary (or even one whose clothes *don't* go together), if you hold every service game, your odds of winning go up greatly; as will your opponent's awe, respect and frustration.

Besides the basic numbers, opponents tend to play less aggressively against first serves than second serves, often assuming that they will struggle to return a first serve. This puts the server with the high first serve percentage in immediate control of the rally after a successful first serve. Like "match", "set" and "sponsorship", "control" is a powerful word in tennis.

On the opposite side of the serving ledger, hitting tons of second serves allows the opponent to feel aggressive; breaks the server's rhythm; is tiring (because you are almost doubling the amount of effort simply to start the point) and is so distracting that it can negatively affect the strokes that follow the serve. Depending on your temperament, it can also be puzzling, maddening or lead to deep, probing and self-destructive on-court stroke mechanics investigations. Sometimes, no, make that, often, a malfunctioning serve can affect every other stroke you hit.

A high first-serve percentage will help the rest of your game stay on track.

COMMANDMENT #2 – Close on the Short Ball

Hitting the ball deep into the opponent's court wins tennis matches. Hitting the ball to the opponent's mid-court (or shorter) is a recipe for losing matches. When your opponent gives *you* the opportunity to win the points by hitting shots to your mid-court or shorter, you need to take full advantage of the opening provided.

It is difficult for most opponents to control the court when they are repeatedly pushed back behind the baseline. They run out of room, hit their responses shorter and have to contend with the back fence. Most recreational players don't have the power to put a ball away from behind their own baseline and the geometry of the court becomes narrower (that is, the angles you can hit to are not as wide) as you move farther back.

However, the geometry of the court becomes wider (that is, the angles open up) as you move closer to the net and/or move wider. Once you move inside the service line (the horizontal line at mid-court), you don't even need to hit a particularly forceful shot to hit a winner. You can create winners through angles and not force. The near-court is a fertile field from which to reap some easy winners. And metaphors.

This second rule and what it asks of your strokes may (and by that I mean *should*) cause you to tweak your practice routine. To take full advantage of mid-court put away opportunities, you will want to (and by that I mean, you will *need to*) learn to hit short pick-up shots off the court (half-volleys); mid-court and near-court volleys; overheads and short backswing groundstrokes off slow, head-height bounces.

Everyone has favorite tasks. Many players practice deep groundstrokes for the majority of their practice time, but never or rarely work to improve these very important mid-court transition shots (volleys and half-volleys) and closing shots (volleys, high mid-court groundstrokes, drop shots and overheads). However, as you begin to witness the pay-offs of mid-court closing shots and understand the importance of these mid-court skills in winning match points, you will naturally adjust how you use your practice time. The acquisition of a few new skills (which may take some time to master) in this area of the court will make you a more effective player.

COMMANDMENT #3 – Hit the Ball Back Three or More Times

Statistically, the average tennis rally during a point in an actual game (and this includes professional tennis) is *five shots*. Not five shots per player, but *five total shots*. I don't know the exact origin of this statistic, but it is widely accepted and despite that is most likely true. Watch a match some time and tally the rally shots and I'll bet you come up with this average, or get a really stiff neck. This means, in the average point, one player hits the ball back two times and the other player hits the ball back three times. Who do you want it to be? You guessed it. *You* want to be the player hitting the ball back three or more times and winning the majority of the points.

How is this done?

First of all, learn to keep the ball in play and get used to medium-length to long rallies. If you can hit the ball back repeatedly, this puts tremendous pressure on your opponent. A recent story on the power-ful Spanish Davis Cup team revealed an unusual training method of the Spanish players. (Besides all of them wanting to be left-handed and play every match on clay.) They stage thousand (yes, *thousand*) ball rallies in practice to be ready for any length rally in an actual match. I'm not suggesting duplicating this feat, but I am suggesting that successful players understand the vital importance of keeping the ball in play.

The statistical story of most tennis matches (even up to the pro level) is not the story of how many winners you can hit, but rather how many *un-forced errors* you or your opponent makes. Yes, that's right. All players lose most of their points by making errors, not by virtue of their opponent's stellar shot making and blistering winners. By being consistent and keeping the ball in play, you let your opponent try over-hard, desperate and imprudent shots. Just the kind you want to see. In short, you don't win your opponent's points for him or her. Instead, by being consistent, you force your opponent to win them themselves. Doing so will increase the amount of your opponent's unforced errors and your points, games and sets.

Learn to love "bludgeon tennis": hitting the ball back repeatedly in one direction. It is an uncomplicated strategy that is an easy way to put this last of the rules into practice on the court. Until you have an obvi-ous chance to change the direction of a shot (you're hit a short ball or a weak ball, or the opponent falls to the court, exhausted from two hours of relentless, repeated, ruthless rallies and gasps, "put the ball away, I've had enough of this ego-bruising comeuppance"), return the ball in the same direction it came from. Complicating this simple strategy not only causes indecision during a point, but can also cause errors as you attempt difficult shots in simple situations. Even more fundamentally, hitting the ball back is as likely as not to allow the opponent to make the error first.

The three commandments are the law of effective and successful match tennis, and as with any boiled-down big ideas, include a host of im-plications about what they mean and how to accomplish them. These three rules will improve you right away and for as long as you play tennis. If the players my son and I watched on that now immortalized August 10 had foregone the many strategies and counter-strategies they entertained and simply re-dedicated themselves to (or even known about) these three guiding principles, all of their matches would have gone a whole lot better. However, they chose mental intrigue, over-strategizing and variable-percentage shot-making and my book-writing began. Save yourself the time and effort of their strategic brain contortions and let the three commandments rule your next match.

GAME TWO – HELICOPTER'S OPTIONAL

(Square The Racquet Face)

"It's hip to be square."

Huey Lewis and the News.

"Hit the ball back three times? Close on the short ball? Navigate the shoals of match competition? It's only game two and already I feel like things are getting out of (racquet) hand. I mean, it all *sounds* simple and helpful, but I still have problems keeping the ball *in the court.* I know you said this isn't a stroke instruction book, but aren't strokes the basis of strategy, isn't pace without depth an empty illusion and isn't a question well-asked half-answered? I need some help here. I want strategy, shot depth and full answers. Before we get to the serve, I need to figure out my groundstrokes."

Groundstrokes are the foundation of any successful tennis game; ground-strokes and hours of practice, good grooming and flexible work hours. They form the edifice of an effective match game, so it's important to understand their architecture. Consistent, reliable groundstrokes give you control over the main elements of hitting and returning the ball. Then other people will want to play with you. If you can maintain and control your groundstrokes *and* can serve, you're ready for match tennis. Then even more people will want to play with you. (At least until you start beating them regularly). Before we build those reliable strokes, a parable –

THOSE WHO CAN'T DO

All instructors should take lessons; especially in activities that are unfamiliar or difficult for them. That way they keep in touch with the feeling of being a student and the struggle that that often (or for me, *always*) implies. Following my own learned counsel, I take golf lessons. One day, at my golf lesson, I asked my instructor for some advice about my backswing. After giving an excellent, simple answer about backswing position, he said, "you know, in a way, it really doesn't matter if you do helicopters at the top of your swing (see: professional golfer, Jim Furyk), as long as you square the clubface on impact." He was right. Right about golf. Right about tennis. Truly a learnable moment. As the saying might go, "One door opens and another – opens."

While you probably don't want to do helicopters during your backswing (although if you hit as well as Jim Furyk, who's to say?), you do want to *square the racquet face* on impact with the ball. To follow two of the three commandments, you need to be able to keep the ball inside the lines when you hit shots off the bounce. Whether you hit flat groundstrokes or topspin groundstrokes, the key to winning tennis and fewer lost balls is keeping your shots *inside the lines*.

FLAT OUT TALENT

Since all variations of flat strokes are based on flat strokes, there is no progressing to big spin strokes until you've attained controllable flat ones. The flat stroke's low to high swing path imparts distance, direction and height cues to the ball. A good drive groundstroke contains two vectors; one traveling straight forward and the other traveling upwards. (Just as a good, well-made sentence often contains the word vector.) Since every well hit ball often needs to be able to travel the length of the court (78 feet from baseline to baseline) and always clear the net (3 feet on center or slightly more on the sides), the recipe for maximum allowable court depth is about eight parts forward swing with the racquet moving about two parts higher at the end of the follow-through.

This all works fine as long as the racquet face is in the same angle relative to the ball on each hit. *Open* the racquet face (tilt the top edge back) on impact and the ball will travel higher and farther than you planned. *Close* the racquet face (angle the top edge down) on impact and the ball will go into the net. Hit with the racquet flat and the ball will follow the stroke line. A predictable racquet angle allows you to perfect and groove your strokes. You know what effect your pace and follow-through are having because these are the only influences on the arc of the shot. An unpredictable racquet angle deceives you. It provides false feedback on what may otherwise be a correctly hit motion. In other words, not because you hit too hard, or didn't bend your knees enough or didn't wear your new nike Court Ballistic 17.2's, but instead because of a few degrees change of racquet angle, your otherwise well-hit stroke can rise up buoyantly and fly impetuously over the fence.

To square the racquet face on impact, lay your wrist back and pay attention to the end cap of your racquet – it should be facing your opponent when your racquet is at full backswing – and not only should this lay your wrist back, the ideal racquet position aligns the string bed perpendicular to the court surface. This will deliver maximum string contact to maximum available optic yellow wool felt ball surface. And that is the most stroke instruction you'll find in one place in this book. I think I can almost promise that.

FIRST THINGS FIRST

An instructional system that puts the additions before the basic stroke is doomed to fail, and fail *you* because it misleads you into doing a lot of hard work to make up for the lack of a solid stroke foundation. Topspin undeniably allows you hit the ball with more force and yet still keep it in the court. And none of what I've said is an attempt to roll back many years of progress in developing the modern, power game. You should add spin to your strokes as your game improves, but initially you need to learn how to hit *through* the ball before learning to hit *over* the ball. In a way, you need to start your stroke apprenticeship in the 1960's to learn how to hit the stroke for the 21st century. Though both hitting through and hitting over are valuable and both are parts of the eventual stroke, it is important to: walk before you can chase down a crosscourt forehand; find the court with your core strokes before you hit between the legs; chat before you pontificate and learn these techniques *in this order*.

On the other hand, if you learn topspin first, you emphasize shots with lots of spin, not with lots of depth. Depth – hitting the ball back into your opponent's court near their baseline – is effective and offense-preserving at any pace. *Depth is the supreme tennis trump card.* Spin, without depth has the same result as a medium-pace flat shot or an accidental account draining deposit delivered conveniently to your opponent: it is an unintended gift.

HOW THE MATCH WAS WON

Control before power. Just enough shot to win the point. These are two of the guiding beacons of enlightened match play tennis. Very few players come off the court after a match loss and lament to their friends, "I wish I'd hit the ball *harder and with more spin.*" (Although I've taught a few who do. They moved on to drag racing, MMA or chainsaw juggling.) What they would probably all acknowledge is that hitting a few more balls *in* would have helped their cause immensely. Very few matches are won purely by power; many are won with control, and all of them are won by not whacking the yellow spheroid out of the court repeatedly; especially at the recreational level. If you're like most players and you have limited practice time, develop a stroke that will hold up even if you're not playing very much. Don't saddle yourself with a stroke that goes on the blink, on the fritz and off the rails if you have to forsake tennis for work for a few days.

And if you decide to use a heavy spin delivery, have a clear idea in mind of what you would like that stroke to look like when it's complete. There is no utility in the recreational game for a shot that clears the net by ten feet and bounds way up in the air off the bounce. First of all, very few clear-thinking, rational, self-interested hitting companions will want to rally with you, because it's not any fun. And any player with a decent volley or overhead will have a fiesta with your pinata set up shots. The shot you eventually want to own is one that accelerates just over the net cord, has the depth to travel baseline to baseline and carries enough topspin that it jumps back at the opponent when it hits the court surface on their side. That stroke is a weapon. Opponents may not like this stroke either – but at least they won't like it for all the right reasons.

This chapter has covered some court, advanced some new concepts and made some big assumptions; in other words, standard confuse-to-clarify protocol. The following list shows what strokes to learn in what order to build the advanced, competitive game many players are paying substantial amounts striving for. If you don't want all of the strokes outlined below and just want to play good recreational or rally tennis, learning the first group will put you on the path to that goal.

THE BASIC ARSENAL – (The Gateway Strokes)

1. Forehand Drive Groundstroke
2. Backhand Drive Groundstroke
3. Serve.
4. Forehand Volley
5. Backhand Volley
6. Overhead
7. Forehand Half-Volley
8. Backhand Half-Volley

Though these strokes are listed in a tidy sequential chronology, you will most likely actually learn #'s 1 – 6 more or less concurrently, with #'s 7 and 8 following. Once all of those strokes are held in your sway and swing, it is time to move to the variations –

THE MORE ADVANCED, COMPETITIVE ARSENAL –
(The Really Addictive Ones)

9. Topspin Forehand
10. Slice Backhand
11. Slice and Kick Serve
12. Drop Shots
13. Slice Forehand
14. Topspin Backhand

With these strokes as well, you may learn them more than one at a time. Remember, all of the most advanced variations begin with solid, flat contact. And that starts with squaring the racquet face. Helicopter's optional.

Groundies grooved. Time for Game Three.

GAME THREE – GUM SHOE

(Connect To The Court)

*"In nature we never see anything isolated, but everything in connection
with something else which is before it, beside it, under it and over it."*

Johann Wolfgang von Goethe

You've squared the racquet face and you're hitting more of the ball
with more of the strings, creating more depth, more pace and more
consistent groundstrokes. This is the first physical step to smarter, better tennis and checks off commandment #3 (Hit The Ball Back Three
Or More Times). To satisfy #'s 1 (Get Your First Serve In) and 2 (Close
On The Short Ball), you'll need a dependable serve and effective closing shots. So far, we've concentrated on the arms. Improvement here
comes from the legs. Just what *is* the rest of your body doing while
the arms swing the racquet? And does it involve leaping, lunging or
springing? Answers may vary.

CAUSE AND AFFECT

Many instructors want their students to emulate the pros. Various
pro-like movements: jumping on serves, leaping and lunging on

groundstrokes and volleys are often uncritically accepted as the *causes* of great stroking. In fact, this may just be a lot of silly cavorting when practiced by the rest of us. These teaching pros honestly think it's a great notion to try to spread this fast, extremely physical style of play to as many people as possible. I think they're making something understandable, but challenging into something obscure and complicated for most recreational players.

Here's one example. I have had students who have been working assiduously during their weekly lessons to develop a solid serve (and learn words like "assiduously"), who then go to a summer tennis camp where an instructor will try to change some of their technique. This pro-technique instructor, who possesses a fabulous if not quite identifiable accent and an equally fabulous, if not quite fully substantiated curriculum vitae will enthusiastically suggest, " You need to *jump* on your serve to get more power!" Student, "Why?" Pro-maker Instructor, "That's what the pros do". That usually settles the issue for the student because he or she senses that the matter is very much settled for that instructor. But is it good instruction? Is it even, properly speaking, instruction? And which pros do they mean? Federer? Serena? Fabrice Santoro? And what about all that assiduousness?

THROWN OFF

The basic physics of a tennis stroke are not hard to figure out. And it is important to ask a few physics questions in order to get useful answers to the jumping/leaping question. The questions are – how is power created in tennis? Is it physical? Is it mechanical? Or is it the size of the endorsement contracts, the entourage and the prize money?

As in just about all other sports, power in tennis is created by storing energy in our body's muscle groups, by a well-timed releasing of that energy and by having a well-connected agent. Initially, when a player prepares the racquet to hit the stroke, they bring the racquet back, turn and bend their knees. The knee bend part happens more or less automatically as the body gets ready to impart force to the ball. This preparation position stores energy in various muscle groups in the body. Once the swing begins, the energy of the arm in motion, the muscular energy of the step and/or rotation of the body are all released to provide power. All of these various forces work *because* the player doing the swinging, transferring weight and rotating starts doing all those things from a fixed point on the court. We commonly call this fixed point the earth. Once any player loses that body-to-earth connection, there may be lots of energy expended but very little useful transfer of energy to the ball. Or, as one of my students famously observed, It's hard to shoot a cannon off a canoe. Hard yes, but accuracy's the real worry.

Consider these examples – the quarterback throwing a pass or the pitcher hurling a fastball. These athletic tasks begin with both feet firmly on the ground. Imagine a quarterback jumping into the air *in order to achieve* better distance and velocity. Imagine a pitcher leaping up and flinging a clutch fastball. When you picture their motions, similar in many ways to hitting a groundstroke or a serve, you realize that though these athletes may move as they release their throw, yet at the critical moment when they begin that release they are driving up and forward *because* they're connected to the ground. It's not that they don't move. They move plenty: just like the pros in tennis. But they are not *in motion* when they create the base for their power. This is the important element connecting the dynamic motions of football, baseball and tennis; as are large paydays and the rote, uninsightful post-game blathering.

The reason the quarterback and the pitcher try to gain as much contact as they can to begin their motion is that if they lose contact to their reference surface (the earth) they have nothing to push against to create their power. (There's that canoe again). No football coach would seriously say to his star quarterback, "You can get more zip on that slant route if you just jump up in the air and then pass." And yet, curiously, there are many players right now who are learning to serve who are taught to jump and hit the ball. They are told that this is a more effective way to hit a hard serve. Not this way, it isn't.

"But what *about* the pros? What is all that leaping and jumping about anyway? If I want to someday hit like they do, doesn't it make sense that I start to do what they're doing?" Of course it does. It all depends on what you mean by doing what they're do. If jumping in the air could make you a professional tennis talent (or even a more skillful recreational player), then why not jump in the air to create that desired level of talent? If it could, then you should. The jumping is the *result* of a lot of drive, practice and hard work on basics. The Pros leave the ground *because* of everything else they're doing. They don't do everything they're doing because they leave the ground. It's just a tiny, understandable mis-construing of all the basic physics behind all tennis strokes; nothing more. Much like saying that the house now burning down caused a terrible fire. As Sir Isaac might say, "Simple mistake. Anybody could have made it."

THE MISSING LINK

The pros get airborne on powerful shots precisely *because* they have connected to the earth *so well* and created so much power, that the force of their connection combined with their body rotation, weight-transfer and stroke speed lift them up. In sports physiology circles this is called the "kinetic link" – the force that drives up from the ground through your body when you create a powerful motion. In everyday speak, we call this being in really good shape and hitting really hard. The incredible torso rotation, swing speed and weight-transfer of the pros' groundstrokes propel them up. In essence (and in every other way), they have pushed so hard they can't stay down. So, in a way, the pro game is a good example of some of the effects you'd like to eventually experience in your own strokes. If your strokes develop to the point where you achieve a spontaneous, Doug-Henningesque levitation (famous '70's magician) as a result, more power to *you* and more power *to* you.

Make sure your base is solid when you begin your serve. A good court connection empowers a powerful serve. If your feet move before you hit, your ball toss accuracy suffers and your moving feet can give unplanned extra momentum to your swing and knock your serve long. A steady foot position will produce a consistent toss, which will in turn produce a consistent serve. I have worked with many advanced players over the years (and even for a few days) who arrive at their first lesson with a serve in disarray and their outlook bleak; despite a well-produced motion, a deep tan and straight teeth. The first adjustment we always consider is for them to stand still when they serve and smile just a little. Once they plant their feet and serve, their percentages instantly rise, their pace improves and their mood lightens.

THE RIGHT APPROACH

Connecting to the court is a vital part of the success of every stroke; groundstrokes, serves, volleys and approach shots. And as you develop moving groundstrokes and midcourt closing shots, it is vital for high percentage shoemaking to get your feet solidly under you before you hit your shot. Connecting to the court creates reliability and power – necessary for moving up and hitting a short ball approach shot or closing shot and directing the ball. You will certainly introduce more movement as your game advances. You may for instance move sooner out of your stance or through some strokes and this is perfectly acceptable.

But all in good time. Occam's Racquet theorem number one is – no points can be scored until you get the ball in the court. Make sure you know how to reliably land the yellow sphere into opponent territory before you step things up by stepping more as you hit. Moving through approach shots or side-to-side shots creates uncertain angles and ball flight at first.

Next time you watch a pro match, spend two or three games just watching *their feet*. Even the players apparently doing the most bouncing and bounding, actually do connect to the court before they hit. They just do it more briefly and recover quicker than the rest of us. But like us, they count their millions one at a time, respect their parents and coaches (often the same person) and run around their backhands. And like us, they still need that connection to begin their violent, asymmetrical slashes at the helpless ball.

When your game is developing, when you are trying to correct an errant stroke mid-career or mid-match or anytime you want to win; make sure that you see the ball, run to get the ball, STOP AND SET UP and then hit the ball. Fret not that you will spend all of your court time rooted as you bash ball. As you net more skills, you will introduce more movement. By grounding yourself in fundamentals, you will end up leaping, spinning and leve-ing your way to airborne felicity. But as with the progression of strokes from flat to top spin, capering, bounding and frolicking are not steps one, two and three when building your technique, but later steps and longer-range rewards for learning and becoming proficient at the basics of sound shot-making.

You want to play like the stars? Start with your feet on the ground.

GAME FOUR – CHANGE LINK

(Master The Transitions)

"Not in his goals but in his transitions is man great."

Ralph Waldo Emerson

If match tennis were only like rally tennis. One or two types of strokes repeated, with each player more or less knowing and therefore anticipating what stroke they will hit next. That would be fun. That would be relaxing. That would be rally tennis. And that wouldn't leave much book to write. One of the great joys of tennis besides an increase in your self-esteem and the improved fit of your jeans, is rallying deep, sweetspot-finding groundstrokes with a friend replying equally skillfully on the far side of the net. But what happens when things get competitive?

WHEN IT COUNTS

Though we've focused so far on molding your strokes into the formidable, relentless and reliable mechanical ingredients of predictable back and forth exchanges, there is another side to the tennis coin; the side that most players need help with – *match tennis*. Tennis where you take the court against an *opponent*; someone who is not trying to find ways to help keep the sphere sailing conveniently and repeatedly but rather someone who wants to end the exchange of sphere *in their favor* as quickly as possible. Someone who, on the court at least, does not have your best interests at heart. Someone who may put you in a tense mental state. Someone who wants to beat you.

If you play match tennis, then you need to master the technique of calling up a variety of different strokes in each point to defeat an opponent. You also need to master the technique of *responding* to a variety of different strokes and situations in each point generated by an opponent. Despite their efforts to be formidable, relentless and reliable, most opponents aren't particularly. To meet the challenges presented by your game and your opponent's game and to please and to tempt the tennis gods and their keen wit, you need to **master the transitions**.

TRANSITORY STATES

But what are the transitions anyway? Transitions as the name suggests, are those times when you are hitting a particular stroke and then change course and hit a different stroke. In rally tennis you are usually hitting one type of stroke (groundstrokes, for instance) against one type of stroke (groundstrokes or volleys). This sort of practice can be beneficial for building stroke technique, rhythm, consistency and a jaunty outlook, but, unfortunately, the very expectation of consistency and predictability doesn't prepare a player for the variety of unpredictable shots, speeds, spins, angles and intentions in real-life-trying-to-win-points tennis match transitions.

<u>Here are some of the most often-encountered match play transitions –</u>

Serve to Groundstroke
Return to Groundstroke
Groundstroke to Volley
Volley to Overhead
Serve to Volley

Transitions require grip, set-up, positioning, swing and attitude changes, all needing to be accomplished in a split second and accurately. And, if possible, stylishly. It is why, if you're intent on succeeding at matchplay tennis, rallying the ball has only a limited usefulness. Rallying will certainly train in stroke steadiness. Unfortunately, it is a rare match that contains mostly deep, well-structured groundstrokes. More often than not, you are barraged by a flock of inconsistently hit responses of varying depth, pace and spin. And that's against a *good* opponent. In an actual match, you often don't know what the next shot will be and yet tennis demands that you be ready for it anyway. This means you need to be prepared to move quickly, set up and hit a different type of stroke than the one you just hit. You need to be able to *make the transitions*. And we're going to examine the big one –

SERVE TO GROUNDSTROKE

The Serve to Groundstroke Transition is the most common transition in tennis, the most important and the most complex. Common because it happens every time you serve the ball in: that is, unless your opponent misses the return, you ace them or you serve and volley. (All really or potentially point-ending options). Important because how well you do it determines how often you hold serve. And complex because it involves the serve, a stroke with a lot of moving parts. Complex also because it involves a quick segue between two dissimilar types of strokes and further complex because it is an occasion when a player should be on offense but often finds him- or herself on defense. It is for those reasons that many players who possess well-developed strokes nevertheless find it easier to win games as receiver than as server; at least at the start of their playing career.

For the transition from serve to groundstroke, as well as match confidence and easier match wins match in and match out, it is important to master the serve. Mastery does not necessarily mean 123.6 mph kick serves wide to the backhand (although if you can un-cork a serve delivery of this magnificence and awe and specificity, do it; often), but it does necessarily mean a first serve that, given your and your opponents' ability level travels at a medium-fast pace and lands inside the opponent's service square seven out of ten times. As a player with a tendency to reach for the glory of the heroic winner at some questionable times, I found it comforting that tennis does not require 100% execution of any stroke. 70% will suffice. So, the serve you want to develop is the one that goes in *at least* 70% of the time. A serve with sufficient pace to put your opponent on the defensive; or at least in neutral and not in full foot on the throttle, hammer back the return mode. A serve that you can direct to different parts of the service square that is reliably successful, purposeful and mechanically repeatable.

The 123.6 mph kick serve (or probably, more realistically, the 77.4 or 86.98 mph delivery with some kick or other perhaps intentional spin on it) that lands in the service box one out of thirty times, but feels great on that one time when it does, is best left for the practice court until it is 70% reliable. By virtue of my own checkered legacy of pursuing a big shot strategy, I know for a fact that big shots rarely win matches. Match tennis is won by high percentage shots. 70% serves.

70% groundstrokes. 70% returns. 70% volleys and overheads. Feel free to be even more consistent, but initially aim for this percentage when vetting a stroke for match play. If most or some portion of your strokes aren't registering this target percentage, play match tennis anyway. Just know that for on-going success, you'll need either high-percentage strokes or a dependable parade of low-percentage opponents.

SERVE TO PROTECT

We discussed it in The Three Commandments; other writers have said it too. Despite all the press, it's still true: *a reliable serve lightens your match tennis outlook*. If your serve isn't landing in, you'll divert valuable mental focus and effort trying to figure out why not. This strain on the sports brain takes energy, saps focus and ultimately leads to reduced effectiveness of all of your strokes. Free your mind by improving your serve.

Secondly, serves are very different from groundstrokes. (In tennis instruction, never shy away from stating the obvious). Serves are hit overhand and are angled down into the court. Groundstrokes are hit low to high, typically up and over the net. (At least on a good day.) Serves are usually hit from a continental or slightly eastern backhand grip. Groundstrokes require a grip change from either of these serve grips. Serves are ideally hit from a stationery stance (see: Game Three) where the server controls all the parts. Groundstrokes are often hit from unbalanced stances or in situations where the hitter is trying hard to establish a solid stance. Groundstrokes are hit after moving to track them down and are largely reactions to the ball that's been hit. And serves are one specific stroke at a time, while groundstrokes have a 50% chance of being on one side of the body and a 50% chance of being on the other. These odds may however vary some or a lot if an analytical opponent notices an extreme weakness on one wing or the other of your game, or you say loudly during the warm-up. "My backhand is really crummy!"

Not only are serves and groundstrokes different, but the expected, predictable and unwavering *randomness* of match tennis requires you to make a quick change from one to the other. In fact, hard serves that are solidly returned can come back extremely fast to the server, further reducing the time available to make this stroke change; thereby quickly turning a potential offensive advantage into "what am I going to do now?" or even into the time-honored, "uh, oh".

Yet, in the undeniable, inescapable, six-segment arithmetic of the tennis set scoring system, if you don't hold (that is, win your own serve, which should be easy), you must break (win your opponent's serve, which is, by design, supposed to be difficult) every time to win sets or matches. But if, instead of climbing the fraught and craggy mount known as repeat service breaks, you serve calmly, deliberately and effectively hold serve every game, you need only win a tie-breaker, or at the most break your opponent's serve twice (depending on who serves first) to win every set you play.

So, therefore, if your serves are not aces, or just plain hard to effectively, successfully return, you must be able to effectively hit the receiver's shot back to their side of the court in order to begin (and win) your own service points. For most players (and even many pros) the reality is that their serve is *not* a weapon, so a high percentage and thoughtful placement of the serve will make it the most effective *set-up shot* it can be. Thought of this way, your serve is just another stroke that along with your groundstrokes, volleys and other game implements is a tool to construct successful points. I know this isn't what the television-celebrated playing professionals do, but until you develop a mighty serve; it is a levelheaded, lower risk way to win matches. By refusing to be enticed by the distracting dream of easy points and consumed by the serve-as-winner mentality as seen on TV, you will avoid the excessive, confidence-robbing second serve attempts that create delicious, eye-widening opponent openings for crushing returns.

Assuming then that your serve is more than likely coming back at you, it's vital to establish your method for taking control of the point from then on. As soon as you successfully make your serve to groundstroke transition, you are most often engaged in a groundstroke versus groundstroke rally and then things get easier. You may even be transported briefly and joyously back to the comfort of something very much like rally tennis. Sometimes a weak, mis-hit, mid-court blooper by the other player tilts this ralleyesque equilibrium to your favor, but typically you should be expecting a solid, penetrating return, and be ready to move in on a short return. The tilting moment can be manipulated to your advantage if you take care of the return of the return. And, so, how do you hit *that shot* effectively and take over the point?

Practice it.

JOB APPLICATION

Just as you have practiced your various stroke skills, you should now practice the serve to groundstroke transition *as a specific skill*. This means that the list of transitions needs to be incorporated into your list of practice items. Match tennis has its own set of skills, based on strokes but often concerned with what you do *between* hitting those strokes. So, in a serve-to-groundstroke practice session, you might do the following–

Start with a basket of balls at your own end of the court and play out some practice transitions. You serve. Your hitting partner returns. And you return that shot. Stop. (Meaning: for this exercise you are only hitting two strokes, and focusing primarily on the transition shot;

the shot you hit after your serve and their return). Then serve again. Return the return. Stop. Serve. Return the return and repeat. You should try various pace serves to various locations and analyze what serves produce the hardest-to-handle returns. If that advice is too advanced at the moment, don't worry, just focus on dropping 70% of your serves in the box and then responding to the serve return. After a few dozen serves to each service square, thank your partner for helping. Or if your partner won't help because he/she only wants to rocket forehands and play like a tennis academy acolyte, find an instructor to do this exercise with. Whichever arrangement you use, make some mental notes as you go. Notice which serves to which locations produce easy set-ups for your point-winning pleasure off the return. (This is a valuable skill for actual match play.) As importantly, notice which serves and returns put *you* in immediate trouble. Avoid these. (As I said, never shy away from the obvious.) Practice this until you can return or put away your practice partner's return 7 out of 10 times. Then switch serve positions and serve to the other side of the court.

Here is one specific technique that will help you prepare to return the return. Learn to take a **split step** after you serve; a stopping step where you run forward, jump and land in a knee's bent ready position. In order to physically and psychologically shift stroke skills, you'll also want to go into a split step position in your home grip (forehand groundstroke) after you serve. This move tells your body and your brain that "we are switching skills." This move also helps you shift from the totally proactive frame of mind of serving to the reactive/proactive frame of mind necessary for hitting groundstrokes.

Your split step should ideally position you on the court to be able to respond to the majority of your opponent's returns. If it doesn't, adjust it. Be adaptable. This may not describe your everyday face-the-world personality, but on the tennis court, in the context of setting up to hit strokes, it will help you. Recovering to a position just behind the baseline after your serve may not cover every type of response shot. Some players return deep into your court, some more shallow. So, start out a match with your split step move positioning you at whatever your transition practice has shown your comfortable return-of-the-return position to be. Then, once you begin to see a depth pattern to your opponent's returns, *adjust your recovery position* to what you receive 70% of the time. (This is another valuable skill for actual match play.) Remember, *no one position can cover the entire court*. Inevitably, you will not be able to return some balls because of the recovery positions you have chosen. But if you make 70% or more from the position you've chosen, you've done very well.

ACTION AT A DISTANCE

Incidentally, it's not always obvious what causes what. (There's a quotation for the ages). What I mean is, not all out balls are poor sphere contact. Not all short ball misses happened because you thought you were "lazy". Not all frumpy opponents have no game. Many times a player makes an error that seems like it was a stroke error, but may actually have been caused by being out of position. You can improve the percentage of any stroke you hit by being in the best position to hit it. The serve to groundstroke transition is perhaps the clearest matchplay example of how much positioning affects stroke percentage. Others of the transitions (with the possible exception of serve *return* to groundstroke) take more experience and therefore more matchplay occasions to analyze. Make the most of the opportunity presented by the serve-to-groundstroke transition – one you can practice in a controlled way. In an actual match, try analyzing your opponent's first ten returns and then begin to adjust your geographic court coordinates.

Other transitions can produce equally dramatic gains once you start to examine and understand them. Though it has been ignored in the pro game for at least a decade, the groundstroke to volley ("approaching the net") transition is not only making a comeback, but is (and has always been) a formidable tactic for recreational players. The mere fact of a live human organism on the other side of the net advancing distracts the other player, foreshortens the court visually for that other player and usually leads to quick points either through opponent nervousness errors or your own dynamic, knife-like slashing volley winners. (Both good options.)

You and your pro should discuss drills and exercises to help you strengthen your awareness and response to the various transitions. (If that avenue doesn't yield any results and you would like some additional transition practice drills, contact me at **marcuscootsona.com**.) Once you integrate stroke transitions into your matchplay, you will not just hit strokes; you will hit *combinations* of strokes. You will, for instance, serve to a certain location, knowing that the return will probably come back to a predictable, agreeable location on your side and give you an opportunity for your follow-up shot.

If, despite the sweeping and sensible advice given above, you prefer not to spend your time on transitions and positioning, but instead just want to rip forehands like a felt-sphere gladiator in dri-fit and get a great cardio workout like a graceful gazelle gamboling on an asphalt veldt, then, by all means, find a like-minded and like-muscled hitting partner and let the felt fly!

If, on the other hand, you want to begin to master the discipline of match tennis, compete to the best of your ability and work towards winning matches in a sustainable way and leave a light psychological footprint, master the transitions. Deft, dependable and eventually dazzling match play will follow for you.

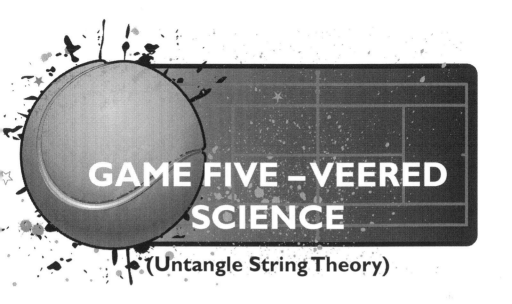

GAME FIVE – VEERED SCIENCE
(Untangle String Theory)

"It's hard to begin to move when you don't know where you are moving, how to move, or if you are going to get there."

Peter Nivio Zarlenga

We are closing out this first instructional set with the urgent intensity of a low-ranked qualifier squeaking into their first Slam draw. Take what you've learned to the court and practice it, and you'll be ahead of the players mentioned at the beginning of this book, most of your tennis friends and a few of your area teaching pros. Your transitions have transitioned, and your body has learned *how* to move to the ball and why and how to stop when you get there. Now it's time to learn *when* to move to the ball; and, as importantly, when to move *away* from the ball. Game Five in our first set is – **String Theory for Tennis.**

Don't worry, it's not just more physics. It's *better* physics. String Theory for Tennis sounds like complicated and obscure quantum mechanics, but it's actually straightforward and clear *movement and positioning mechanics.* String Theory in physics is one single theory to explain everything. String Theory for Tennis is one single theory to explain where to be when on the playing surface, and how to know when to be where: a conceptually simpler goal but only slightly easier to pull off.

EDUCATED AND REFINED

As you construct your complete match game and play more competitive points, games and sets, you may find yourself asking these questions: How do I know *when* to move to cover a short shot? How do I know when to retreat on a deep shot or approach for a winner? Face an array of opponents with a variety of games styles and hitting techniques, and you develop an unconscious mental archive of how to move and when to move. This unconscious downloading of match data can take a while to accumulate, so we're going to give the unconscious some conscious direction and, in the process, speed this process along.

ANALOGISM

I teach a young woman – great forehand, slice backhand, strong serve (though the toss is a little too high), world-class speed, modified German accent – we'll call Steffee. (Not her real name. Real name is Stephanie.) She likes her groundstrokes, especially her forehand; and she is most secure staying back and blasting bombs from the backcourt. There is nothing inherently wrong with her game plan and yet there are certain situations for her, and for all level players, even those with only neighborhood-class speed, where coming to the net would be the most efficient way to win the point. She and I have been working on adding net play to her game. I'm convinced she needs it. She thinks she might want to be convinced. So, we often play practice points and then review them for improvements. Here's a sample –

It is mid-point. Steffee and I are gunning groundies and our positions on the court are neutral (that is, neither one of us is advancing or retreating and no political affiliation is expressed) and for the moment the best thing we can both do is to stay where we are and not approach the net. During our exchange, however, Steffee uncorks a big forehand deep into my forehand corner, pushing me back from the baseline and off to my right. As I backpedal quickly and respond with a loopy, defensive forehand medium-deep back to her, I watch for a change in her court position, but true to her instincts, she stays put near her baseline and the rally continues. I recover my baseline position; find a way to hit the ball to her backhand; push her back; come to the net and finish the point with a short, angled volley. She mutters something in German. I don't think it was "nice shot".

We deconstruct the point and it becomes clear to Steffee that the deep forehand that pushed me back should have functioned as an *approach shot*: a time to make an offensive move forward and take control of the net. However, as this point was actually developing, there was no inner stirring of her unconscious tennis geist that beckoned her to come to the net. In fact, given her reliance on the power and intimidation of her baseline game, my desperate position probably made it seem like a great time to tough it out from where she was. (Many of her opponents can be felled in such a situation by her power off the deep stroke.) In any event, her unconscious tennis mind wasn't yet directing the action. It takes many more examples for a player to truly integrate an unfamiliar strategy like the one I'm asking of Steffee. There's nothing wrong with this inductive method – playing points, analyzing the components of the exchange and highlighting areas to improve – but like learning Armenian underwater, it can be slow going.

FRAMING THE WORK

Instructors, tennis writers and helpful playing partners advise that when you see the opponent's feet moving backward from the baseline or off the court on either side, that this is the time to approach the net or put away the ball. Others say that certain types of shots – approach shots, first volleys, half-volleys, deep-angled groundstrokes, drop shots and lobs – should always be followed up by coming to the net. I agree. But what's the general rule, or theory or incantation that connects all of these specific cases? One day, mid-rally in a playing lesson with a student named Andray (not his real name) (real name is Stan), it struck me that there's another way to know when to move forward and when to move back. And that's the day I notioned up, **String Theory for Tennis.**

Stay with me, 'cause it's about to get all theoretical. Imagine that you and your opponent (or you and your hitting partner) are connected by a very long string. So far, every bit as wacky as "real" String Theory. And being imaginary, the string is less than fully visible. In fact, it is *in*visible, but still strong enough to be felt (at least by those who believe), yet weak enough to break without too much tension. The string not only connects you, it also helps to keep Player Personal Distance (PPD) on the court. PPD on the tennis court is much the same as personal distance in social settings. It is the appropriate amount of distance between you and another person: in this case, the appropriate amount of distance between you and your opponent. To stay connected and maintain the proper PPD, the imaginary string should always be taut. If it's too taut, it will break. And if it's too loose, it will stop working. This imaginary string will stay taut as long as you keep the same distance from the player on the other side of the net.

EVENTS THAT MOVE YOU

If an opponent moves back three feet, you move forward three feet.

If they move back and to the side six feet, you approach the net six feet.

If the opponent bounds over the net wildly brandishing their racquet and quacking irately about some long-forgotten line call, run!

This is the basic notion of String Theory for Tennis; definitely a smaller weird-o-meter reading than Edward Witten imaginary physics. This theory would have helped Steffee in our practice point. As soon as I moved back and to my right, she should have felt pulled in to the net by the amount I moved back. This would have given her the position to hit an approach shot and move forward to the net.

READING THE SIGNS

It's no secret (or is it?) that our eyes work better tracking an object like a tennis ball *across* our visual field (that is, from right to left, or left to right), than they are tracking an object coming at us. Everyday, players of all levels misjudge how shallow some shots will land on their side. Without a lot of data from matches, speed and depth movements and responses are often guesses.

However, with experience, or a really expensive com link to your swing advisor, it is possible to know, based on the opponents' body language, racquet position and swing speed as well as solidity of contact, where a ball will land: and whether it will be deep or short. Still, like the other features of unconscious learning, intuiting your spouse's needs and the two- or three-letter words in the Scrabble Dictionary, this knowledge can take a long time to acquire. By using String Theory for Tennis, you can make some educated guesses about where the ball will touch down on your side of the court; even if you can't visually tell its depth from how it's been struck.

If your opponent is pushed two feet behind the baseline to hit a ground-stroke, move inside the baseline two feet. Why? Since the opposing player has been pushed back, their stroke will most likely be weaker and more shallow. You now have a better chance to reach what will most probably be their shorter response shot.

If your shot allows your opponent to move into the court by three feet, chances are they are going to step in and hit the shot very deep to your backcourt. No need to guess if the ball might be deep in your court, assume that it will be. Move back three feet, respond to their shot: and look composed and in control doing it.

This kind of subtle adjusting also works when the opponent shifts even a teeny, tiny distance forward or back; maybe for balance or footwork reasons *they* don't even understand. Not only does it mean you are staying awake and alert and ready as you continually factor your opponent's position into your set up, it means also that you are moving your feet between shots and working to set up early in each shot.

CALIBRATING THE INDIVIDUAL

To make String Theory for Tennis work in match play, you need to decide *for each opponent that you play* on the optimal PPD for groundstroke rallies, volley to groundstroke exchanges and after-match socializing. This calculation may take a few games (or more) to establish and may even change as your opponent warms up, then tires out and ultimately grows despondent, taciturn and pathologically morose as the score mounts in your favor. Like other tactics such as serve speed, your mix of defense vs. offense and choice of headband, shirt and shoes, what really matters is that for each opponent you measure the PPD early and decide how much space you ideally want to have between you and them. Once you figure this out, String Theory for Tennis can help you maintain that PPD on every shot of every point.

Outside air temperature affects how high and how far a tennis ball bounces and this can alter your calculations also. Some students say this sounds like an excuse. Now there are excuses and there are explanations; the defining difference besides spelling is the amount of whining used to describe something. And physics is physics, as the philosophers say, and temperature has a big effect on ball bounce. If the air temperature is between 65 and 75 degrees Fahrenheit, the ball will bounce just as its maker intended. At lower temperatures the ball will begin to fly shorter and deflect lower off the court surface. On cold or cold/damp days, your PPD will be *shorter*. At higher temperatures, the ball will travel farther and bounce higher off the court surface and the PPD will be *greater*. Even knowing this, start the match from your usual distance and then after observing the effects of temperature on the velocity and depth of your opponent's shots, begin to adjust the string.

What about serves and returns? String Theory for Tennis plays here too. The serve return calculation is a little different from that for groundstrokes and volleys, however. Here the speed of the opponents' serve will suggest your PPD from them. This will obviously take a few serve rotations to figure out, but after a few-games' sampling of the opponent's point starting style, you will begin to find the distance. Many players can be very good at this skill and still be flummoxed by slow second serves. Consider the first serve speed to be the speed at which the string is taut, then imagine that a slower second serve shortens the string and move farther into the court. This works much the same as adjusting to the short ball.

In String Theory for Tennis, we strive for perfect tautness. This suggests that some positions can be too loose and some can be too taut. Too loose happens when you opponent moves back six inches and you approach by eight feet. Here, the opponent has not really been forced back into a defensive position and will have a good opportunity to hit a shot behind you, because you have let the string slack too much. Or, if the opponent moves forward two feet and you retreat ten feet. The string is now too taut and will break. By breaking the string connection, you have disturbed the balance you wanted to maintain and have left yourself open to an easy drop shot. No need to let that happen.

FOR EVERY ACTION

Much of String Theory for Tennis develops naturally for players with substantial match experience. But even advanced or expert players can use help developing better positioning instincts. Seeing the tennis court give-and-take as a variation on tug-of-war can tell you where the opponent is likely to move when you hit a particular shot that alters their court coordinates. Predicting their move in response to your shot can give you the opportunity to anticipate their next setup position and even give you the opportunity to confound them by approaching or retreating at unconventional times.

The flip side of String Theory for Tennis is *using* your relative depth in the court to influence the type and depth of shot your opponent chooses to hit. Roger Federer has developed his own, expert version of court positioning as a tactical weapon. Federer varies his baseline position in most rallies on almost every shot in what seems to be an effort to put the imaginary string in constant flux. He thereby forces his opponents to continually adjust their own positions and expectations based on where he moves. He has been praised repeatedly by commentators for his skill in turning defense to offense; always, however, in the area of shot making. I think his elaborate, calculated baseline re-positioning is another, more subtle means to the same goal.

What about those times when your opponent advances into their near court, but executes a too-short approach shot that forces you to approach and thus compress or tangle the imaginary string? Fear not, there are special cases in almost any theory, no matter how elegant, comprehensive or conclusive. That certainly is the case in a sport with as many physics principles in play on each point as the game of tennis. Advice in this case – jettison the theory and get to the net immediately. After all, it is just a theory. *String theory is there to control your PPD to your opponent when you are both near the baseline.* As soon as one player has taken up a position at the net, cover the angles, look for the opponent's tells and put away the ball. The string got you this far, now tie up your opponent with it.

This is the final physical game pillar in the match game edifice. Play with these five games in your game, and just like Steffee and Andray (not their real names), you will avoid the physical stumbling blocks many players put in their own way, and you will be on your way to improved match tennis and the next chapter. You are now a better wizard. Before we leave the physical game for a higher Chakra, let's talk wands.

GAME SIX – TOP GEAR

(Play With Good Gear)

"Man must shape his tools lest they shape him."

Arthur Miller

Okay, final game of the first set. We've scorched the lines for some tennis theory winners; finding not only the simplest, smartest ways to pelt the felt, but also how to move, how to move between moves and how to know when to move when you do move. Our devious, energy-sapping opponent – complicated, thoughtless tennis – is barely hanging on. Bill Ockham is shooting us air high-fives and offering heartfelt, terse compliments. Verging on a commanding first set win, we still need one more game to finish it off and advance to the deciding second set. This final physical-set game is all about the most physical part of the sport of tennis– **The Gear**.

WHEN BAD GEAR HAPPENS TO GOOD PEOPLE

To play tennis, you need the gear. To play good tennis, you need the good gear. Most players know this in their heart of rational hearts, yet many players game their games by wearing the wrong clothes, playing in inappropriate shoes or worse yet, wielding a weak and weary racquet. Why? Because Tennis – the establishment and the activity – doesn't call them on it. Clubs, leagues and tournaments have abandoned their dress codes and most players are only too happy to comply. And that's just the esthetic part. What about the playing multitudes using old, wrong or useless racquets? You may be tempted to blame it on the economy, but this sad equipment trend predates the Great Recession and will someday be traced to a defective piece of human tennis DNA.

Players throughout the tennis nation content themselves with junky tennis equipment and sell themselves and their tennis egos short by wearing visit-to-the-grocery-store sportswear, droopy bottom cargo bottoms and gamey old t-shirts on court. Why? Mostly, because they can. Still, as a bumper sticker once so rightly observed, "just because you *can*, doesn't mean you *should*". Think about lycra for a moment. Or, vehicles of a certain size. Or those lobe-hugging cell phone earpieces. Briefly de rigeur items of dubious cultural value that citizens of discretion and discerning appearance may want to avoid. Same story with sub-standard sports stuff. Avoid it, and play better.

Tennis is a sport. But, even among sports, the consequences for messing up are minimal. In sharp contrast to sports like horseback riding, bungee jumping, skydiving, scuba diving or car racing (to name a few), tennis typically has no life or death consequences. In tennis, a bad outcome is not enjoying your hitting session, losing your match or whiffing a floater overhead at the club show court or on an important first date. Unlike a bad day auto racing or skydiving, at the end of the session, you're still alive (though perhaps dining alone). That's why a tennis instructor can send you on the kind of self-destructive path (see; some earlier chapters and numerous harangues) that would get a flight instructor or driving instructor sued and/or jailed. In tennis, the consequences of bad instruction like those from bad equipment are not so obvious.

This lack of life or death consequences leads many players to use improper gear – gear that in an activity where every detail either promoted or discouraged survival and limb retention could be disastrous. Since it is possible to play with inadequate equipment, many players do. Often the justification is, "I'm not good enough yet to get good equipment. The good stuff, that's for *real* tennis players."

But, my friends, I ask you to consider for a moment; does it make any sense to take lessons, read books, practice and think carefully about the game if there is one looming obstacle keeping you from playing as well as you can? Some players feel that blaming poor play on equipment is a crutch. A lot of these same players feel that playing better with that "crutch" is also unfair. While it is true that no equipment can make you better, it is also true that some equipment can make you worse.

What if you took up a *dangerous* activity? What if your sport were skydiving? Would you want an old, worn-out parachute or one that was new and fully functioning? Of course you'd want the one you knew would work. (If not, I have some people you can call. They'll help.) This is because its function makes a difference. I'll bet the same athletes spurning good tennis gear wouldn't refuse the functioning parachute or dismiss it as training wheels for novices. It would (properly) be viewed as a necessity. To skydive without incident and to remain intact to skydive again, you want the proper gear. To play tennis without incident and to attract enthusiastic, repeat hitting partners, you need the proper gear.

OCCAM'S RACQUET

IT'S ALL ABOUT YOU

Think for a moment what using lousy stuff says about your sports self-image. It says you don't think much of your prospects for success and it sends a self-fulfilling, negative message to your strokes. I'm reminded of the golfer (a composite of many I've played with), who facing a tee shot over an imposing water hazard, takes out an old ball, figuring that the ball may go in the water. And guess what? With that pre-shot attitude, it often does. Since so much of what leads to sports success is pre-determined by the player's attitude, turn this negative to a positive and reject the self-fulfilling fatalism. When you're golfing, take out your best ball and *intend* to hit it over the water. In tennis, suit up, gear up, person up and plan to play well.

If you are a tour pro, you can ignore this next part. And if you are, I'm flattered that you're reading my book. If I didn't mention you in any of the examples, it was an oversight. I'll correct it in the next edition. So, skip to the next paragraph and enjoy! If you are a recreational player, you are precisely the person who needs to read this: **you need good equipment**. A skilled professional might be able to play in jeans with running shoes, a $25.00 racquet and worn out tennis balls, because they can compensate. They might be able to, but they *wouldn't*. They know the advantages of using the good stuff. What about the rest of us without pro-level skills? We need everything to be as helpful to our particular game as possible. Our games already have more variables than we're aware of. We don't need to add any. We require our equipment to do what it's supposed to do so that we will know what effect our efforts are having. If your equipment is variable and your strokes are also variable, it's very difficult to know exactly which variable is affecting the outcome.

A more practical pitch for good gear is this – you can probably afford it. Put another way, can you really afford *not* to afford it? Compared to the gear needed for other sports and activities, tennis equipment is relatively inexpensive. For instance, a can of the best quality tennis balls is less than a designer Latte. Of course, there's more to affording the full kit of tennis gear than tennis balls; and that's a relief to tennis retailers. You see, in an ironic and self-destructive master bumble of industry marketing, the tennis manufacturing powers-that-be have structured it so that there is no retailer profit in retailing tennis balls. Selling lots of them only makes the loss per can into a larger, aggregate loss. Take advantage of the industry's arithmetic impairment and buy tennis balls often. For most tennis players, the single greatest inexpensive tennis gift they can give themselves is new tennis balls. Unlike some wines, all yogurt and most jokes, they don't get better with age. Once you open a can of tennis balls, play with them for one session and then recycle them or play fetch with the pooch. It is not practical, humble or virtuously economical to keep old tennis balls. It is detrimental, morally irrational and damaging to our strokes and our sports self-esteem. (I guess that makes my opinion pretty clear.)

Let's now consider the categories of equipment the retailers *do* make some money on, and what that equipment is supposed to do–

THE RACQUET

The racquet is the most conspicuously essential equipment element, so we'll start there. Racquets basically come in three head sizes – mid-sized, mid-plus and over-sized. (Why do the sizes start at *mid*-sized? Long story. Next book.) Sounds simple, but the amount of choices available can be staggering; and even when it's not staggering, it's darn confusing. It might seem that the stores like it this way. They don't. Confused customers don't buy. They walk. After selling tennis racquets for thirty years as a retailer in my own stores and at professional tournaments, my associates and I found that there was one simple question that helped point us in the right direction when assisting a customer with racquet selection. That one question was – "How many do you want?" (no, that wasn't it). "Would you like a warm-up, four tops, three bottoms, new shoes and socks with that?" (That wasn't it either). Now I remember. Our racquet question was – **"what length swing do you have?"** Any player's answer to this one simple question told us much of what we needed to know in order to help them select a suitable stick.

Our simple suggestion to their answer was that the *bigger* your swing, the *smaller* racquet you should consider. If you use a long, traditional swing and the swing itself generates power, a mid-sized racquet will add control to your power. If your swing is medium-length, look at mid-plus racquets and consider over-sized or super-over-sized racquets if you have a short swing. If you're uncertain how to characterize your swing, either buy one of each size racquet (a retailer-endorsed idea) or ask your tennis instructor to tell you (probably simpler and cheaper).

Our one-question-fits-all inquiry was useful because it is applicable to players almost irrespective of their ability. While many beginner's underdeveloped strokes are short, some beginners have long, powerful strokes. Most advanced players use a long swing motion, but not all of them do.

The basic guideline to racquet size selection is this: *bigger racquets have more power and smaller racquets have more control*. The advertising from the racquet companies, the advice from various partisan industry blogs and the opinion of your buddy who's read a lot of reviews may attempt to convince you otherwise, but this principle holds unavoidably. It's just physics, and physics isn't persuaded by marketing.

GAME SIX – TOP GEAR

Racquets are made of various materials and composites; many of them unpronounceable, some of them superfluous and all of them lighter and stronger than last year's. Once you've found a racquet size category, look for the other factors that influence how it plays. They include: how thick the beam of the racquet is when viewed side-on (thicker frames tend to play stiffer than thin ones); how stiff or flexible the frame is (stiffer frames typically have more control, flexible frames have more power): what it's made of and maybe as important– how it looks when you hold it. By all means, don't disparage good graphics. You need to *believe* that you can play well with a racquet to use it successfully.

How much is "affordable" anyway? Currently, new state-of-the-sport racquets retail below $200.00. And, as I mentioned, tennis balls cost the dealer more than they cost you. The core items that get you started and keep you playing are about as much as three lift tickets, four green fees or a tire. But, if even this amount of money sounds intimidating, and you're tempted to use a hand-me-down racquet that's been in the garage for decades, please don't. Spend the money. If you want to pursue this great sport, do yourself and your tennis ego the honor of using serviceable equipment. Don't let unwieldy gear stand in your way. The hand-me-down, garage-stored racquet has dead strings; the frame has lost its kick (after the first five years or two hundred hours of play) and it is heavier and higher in vibration than today's racquets. (And that's the *positive* pitch). A new racquet, fitted specifically to your game will be more maneuverable, more powerful and will control the ball better. Go to a knowledgeable pro shop or specialty shop, try some demos, ask questions, try some more demos and then buy a racquet that complements your game.

(If all of this is too confusing, too general or if you simply want some more detailed, personal advice, please e-mail me at **marcuscootsona.com**.)

THE SHOES

My advice? You guessed it. Wear tennis shoes for playing tennis. Tennis shoes are specifically designed for tennis; running shoes, walking shoes and casual shoes are not. Tennis shoes are tailored for lateral support; their wider outsole design helps you stay stable and injury free as you move side to side and up and back on the court. A tennis hard court surface is typically very grippy (that is, there's a lot of friction between shoe and court surface) and running shoes, while they may be light and fast, are generally not laterally as stable. Their edges can catch and their thinner soles can roll over easily, leading to possible ankle and foot injuries. Walking shoes and casual shoes are unfitting for most of the same reasons and just look dorky.

Also, tennis shoes are made to take the pounding of a hard-court surface and are constructed to stand up against the abrasion of a hard-court surface. And they make you look like a committed tennis player; not like a tennis player who should be committed. The amount you pay for a good pair of tennis shoes will be repaid to you in support, long wear, lack of injury and general comfort and spiffiness.

THE CLOTHING

No secret as to my opinion here. Respect the game. Wear tennis clothes. No, it doesn't mean you're a poser or a wannabe or a screaming dilettante if you do. It means that you're dedicating yourself to the game you're playing. It means that even if you're just beginning, you are giving yourself every means to improve at the activity you've chosen. It means you are putting yourself in the frame of mind to succeed at what you're doing. You are not out at the track, in the gym, shopping for dinner or gardening, you are on a tennis court and you came to play.

On a more practical note, the obvious reason to wear tennis clothes is that they are made for tennis. Tennis tops are typically made of moisture-wicking fabrics that are cut to provide movement for tennis. Tennis shorts and skirts typically have room to hold tennis balls to help with practice rallies and second serves.

CLOSING AGREEMENTS

It's seductive to think, "If I dress like I'm not really a player, then no one will judge me as one and they won't see the flaws in my game." Seductive, yes. True to a certain extent, yes. But, it's a fustian bargain (Not from Faust, but from fusty) you've made. People won't think you're a tennis player, but ask yourself – if you're not a real tennis player now, when will you be? When your backhand gets better? When your team wins its league championship? When you get your first ATP point? Or ask yourself this – when is the first day of the rest of your tennis life? The answer is of course – *right now*. Whenever you go to a tennis court to play, you are a tennis player with whatever ability you have. When you convince the spectators that you're not really a player, you are also convincing the one person who matters most in the equation that you're not really a player. And that person is *you* the player. Then, sadly, that first day of the rest of your tennis life also gets pushed off one day later. Not only do they say in Latin, "Carpe Diem!" (Seize the day!) They also say, "adepto vestry nonnullus bonus apparatus!" (Seize some good gear!)

Embrace and own your talent at every level. Rejoice in your improvements and your victories as you move up in ability. And since I know that by reading this book you have proven that you're serious about taking steps to improve, learn the physical game and play it with good gear. To paraphrase an old coaching chestnut, "Failing to gear up is gearing up to fail."

When you combine what you know about the physical game with the confident attitude made possible by proper outfitting and positive on-court demeanor, comportment and appearance, you've won the first set in the battle for better tennis, 6 – 0. Now, you're on the way to taking this match in straights. Let's take a break. The changeover from the physical to the psychological game is a good time to hydrate, have a banana or an energy bar, look adoringly at your new racquet, change into one of your new outfits and mentally prepare for the brain workout to come. It's time to serve to start the second set!

THE SECOND SET

LET'S GET MENTAL

(The Psychological Set)

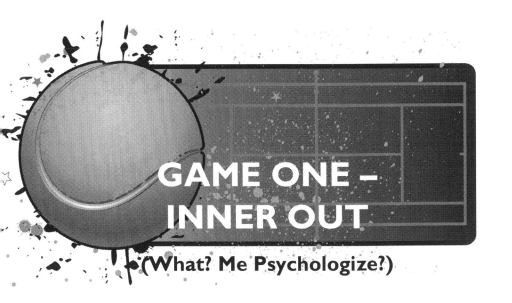

GAME ONE –
INNER OUT
(What? Me Psychologize?)

"Idleness is the parent of psychology."

Friedrich Nietzsche

The physical set is now in the books. For the record, simple, intelligent tennis cruised through complicated, thoughtless tennis 6 – 0. But fortunately or unfortunately one set doesn't finish an opponent and the best strokes don't always win; otherwise match results would be very different worldwide. If stunning ball striking was everything, then tennis would be easier to master and far less interesting for intelligent adults; the groomed and grooved stroke artist would always beat the no-technique-do-anything-to-win pusher, the sport would be dominated by NBA defectors and Marat Safin would have won 53 Grand Slams. Twice. However, the physical game isn't all of the game. In fact, it's not even half of the game. You certainly can't play without it, but you can't *win* consistently without a sturdy, dependable *mental game.*

Though the mental game of tennis is the second half of this book, it's much more than one half of the thinking player's arsenal. As some tennis wag once witicized (Yogi Berra with me here), "Tennis is 90%

mental and the other 50% is mental." The arithmetic is as shaky as ever, but the analysis is still about 139% valid. There's an obvious and challenging physical dimension to the game (otherwise, what were the last six chapters for?), but in order to play great *match tennis* at any level, you have to understand the mental game. Does that mean sports psychology? Well, yes and no. And maybe. It all depends on what is meant by sports psychology. To make this at least as clear as the Davis Cup format, let me introduce you to my junior tennis coach.

MASTER CLASS

I was taught the game of tennis by a well-rounded coach, although personally he was quite fit and slender. If his parents had just a little more sense of destiny or irony, his name might have been something like Al Agory; but it wasn't. However, to protect him from Reality TV offers and TMZ paparazzi, we'll just call him Coach Al. Coach Al was a renaissance athlete and sports theorist, having played and coached more sports than most people had tried and quit. He taught me tennis, but he could easily have schooled me in football, basketball, baseball, golf or boxing. Though the technical requirements are unique, tennis is a sport that has many of the same prerequisites as all ball sports; a basic sprinkling of athletic gifts, some coordination and tracking skills and indulgent parents or other financial sponsors willing to pay for lots of coaching and instruction. Principles of good technique, good practice habits, sound mental approach (even if you are not completely sound mentally) in one sport can lead to success in others. Although, even those things don't guarantee a killer topspin backhand half-volley.

For Coach Al, all sports were a system of self-improvement, self-discovery and self-mastery based on physical skills. And though we talked about my tennis for three hours a day, five days a week for four years (so went my youth), we never discussed whether or not I was going to go pro. His teaching was all about personal excellence and self-discipline. Of course, with that kind of naïve, classicist approach he would be ridiculed, ignored and probably un-employed today.

In Al's world, all ball sports were about a few basic things. First, you need a ball, a playing area and an opponent. Beyond that: you need to play the ball, not the other player; get position on the ball early and then take your shot or make your stroke. And since when the legs and the center of gravity go, technique suffers, you need leg strength and core strength. Therefore, my hitting partner and I endured vast quantities of running and strength training; sometimes willingly. All right, mostly willingly; but still with enough moaning and resistance to be fully credible teenagers. It did pay off in matches, though. You could be a great ball striker, but you in order to win you have to strike the ball well for three sets. Whatever our talent level was, we could go the distance with it.

On the tennis court, Coach Al's actual instruction was sparse, even cryptic sometimes; yet there was always a purpose to it. He was reasonable, urging and demanding. But he was never loud, never angry, never belittling, and always interested in the goal of developing positive self-image. He was so expert and yet so calm at what he did, that I suspect that no "fabulous", "champion producing", "hit like the pros" tennis academy worth its blustering, self-aggrandizing press releases would even consider him today. And what would he think of them?

THERE IS NO SUCH THING AS SPORTS PSYCHOLOGY

I think he was up on the latest sports and tennis theories. Even if he wasn't, he always had an opinion about them. Still, I was a shocked jock to hear one afternoon's practice court pronouncement. I had an important match coming up against a highly-ranked, highly-regarded player and I wanted to quell some nervous apprehension about facing him. Me, "What should my psychological approach be?" He, "**There is no such thing as sports psychology.**"

Mind you, this was back in the early 1970's; the era of Jimmy Connors, Stan Smith and Ilie Nastase, really small wood and metal racquets and tennis as sport fad du jour. Our equipment was more impediment than advantage, and we all needed help where we could find it. Many players thought they had found it in the emerging field of sports psychology. Americans (even teenage tennis groms) were just beginning to hear about a new set of theories that promised a better way to peak athletic performance. W. Timothy Gallwey's *The Inner Game of Tennis* was very popular, and sports psychology was one of the many religions proliferating at the time. Gallwey's call to free your inner, intuitive player and suppress the rational, critical, analytic brain spawned a new way of thinking, or at least of feeling and intuiting about the game. It also gave inflated false hopes to thousands of players who didn't really want to work at or get real sweaty developing rigorous, technically-sound tennis strokes. Still, as *The Inner Game...* became popular, it even led many serious players to try to sort out their sports mojo and the game between the ears. I was looking for some of this new alternate athletic dogma to help me. But instead of GPS points for the road to the new sports truth, my coach gave me nihilism. Or so I thought.

What did Coach Al Agory mean? And, whatever he meant, did he *really* mean it? Was this some kind of Pre-New Age parable? Was it a test? If he did mean it, was it true? And, if it was true, was this budding industry the work of quacks and charlatans? Was he trying to be provocative? Was this an ontological statement? Was I reading too much, too little or not quite enough into his cryptic commandment? And, what about the "Inner Game"? This was a theory written and published long before the viral flowering of self-publishing. e-books and Wikipedia. In those bygone times, we assumed published words were properly vetted by some authority and were true. What about Gallwey's words? Didn't they *have* to be true?

Obviously, I had lots of questions.

THERE IS HOWEVER SPORTS *PHILOSOPHY*

Like the student-athlete I thought I was, I reasoned it through from the beginning; taking clues where I could find them from Coach Al's other categorical statements and subtle pronouncements. And so as not to give my fourteen year-old self too much credit, I don't think the answer became clear until much later.

But back to the past. Starting with a first premise is the time-tested, laborious, logic 102 way to construct a sound argument. But I did it anyway. I needed to find Coach Al's first principle of his sports philosophy and this seemed like the best way to reveal it. Since he was a strong believer in positive mental attitude, I took this as his axiom. In fact, upon deep teenage reflection – probably 10–15 minutes – I came to see that his sports *philosophy* was this: our minds can only understand and use statements as if they were *positive reinforcements*. He would view today's sports psychology encouragement of "positive self-talk" as a redundancy; for him there was only one mood for inner monologues: positive. In his version of peak sports performance, statements like, "I can't miss this serve" are worse than useless. They convey the negative concept of missing and give it power as it is affirmed. Coach Al's point was that when we are in a simple fight or flight setting (such as the tennis court or the playing field), our brains can only hold and use messages in the positive. He didn't know it, but he was an unknowing visionary.

In high stress, fight-or-flight settings, our higher reasoning processes shut down to protect us by not distracting us with abstract thoughts in situations – game shows, gladiatorial contests, DMV appointments – that demand maximum physical alertness and resources. We therefore need specific, positive statements such as "I *will* hit this serve in." "I *see* this serve going in." "I *will* hit the apex of the lines with this on-the-run-open-stance-down the-line backhand screamer to save triple match point". Affirmations like this help us by giving our minds something usable and useful to process; a pursuit of all that is positive, instead of just an avoidance of an unwanted negative. The lesson was that the negative you think or speak becomes real and really negatively affects your sports performance. So, yes, Coach Al was a yes-man from way back.

THE OUTER GAME

But when it came to the notion that sports psychology could some-how transform us into players with abilities we didn't previously have, unlocking technical proficiency we had not yet acquired and make us into tour-pro-style match winners; he found this position impossible to support, or, as I see it now, difficult to even comprehend. So, I pressed him about what his no-sports-psychology statement really meant. He looked at me, paused and thought for a moment. Then, as if articulating for the first time what he'd always known intuitively (but in reality had probably been waiting for me to ask), he proceeded with this two sentence "clarification" of his one-sentence proclamation – *"You are either better conditioned than your opponent or you aren't. You either hit more balls in the court than your opponent or you don't."*

Okay, that was potentially more explicit and more specific, but what did it mean? He had often said, "Play the player, not his ranking" and "Don't look at the draw sheet before a match" and memorably, "An army runs on its stomach"; which I must admit, always sounded anatomically difficult and darn painful. But what did conditioning and stroke consistency have to do with the game of the *mind*? That was all I ever really got from Coach Al on the subject. Though a philosopher by inclination, he wasn't much given to speculation or explanation.

I convinced myself that I partially understood what he meant at the time. Hit well and be able to run all day. That wins matches. But what about Gallwey and mojos and the critical 140%? The answer bubbled up from an unlikely wellspring some years later. I was talking with an opera singer friend a few days before a performance at an important and imposing opera house. I asked her if she thought she might get nervous performing. She answered immediately, "No, not if I've practiced. I only get nervous if I don't know what I'm doing." She said this years after my coach's bold statement and inscrutable semi-clarification, but her comment and attitude re-rang some important approach-to-the-mental-game memory chimes. I found myself reflecting on the Coach Al Agory proverb. I realized that just like my opera singer friend's idea that preparation trumped nerves; that the no-sports-psychology proposition was a sound, practical framework for handling the mental aspect of a tennis match and not just a dismissive brush off on a hot practice court by a man who always made us work for the meaning of his words. (And, who knows, maybe like any prophet, he didn't always know exactly what he meant, either.)

RESERVOIR DOG OF KNOWLEDGE

Here's how the Coach Al Agory no-sports-psychology philosophy has played out over the millennia I've been teaching (I know I *look* younger) – if you want to be in the frame of mind to win a tennis match (at any level), you must be focused and positive and confident. We'll focus our focus on focusing and confidence in a literary moment. Right now, let's zoom in on how to be positive. Being positive on the tennis court means knowing exactly what shots you can make and what shots you can't make. Knowing your abilities and your limits informs your on-court choices. Knowing what you can and can't pull off tells you how to handle your opponent's spins, speeds, angles and attitudes. You don't need to decide on an approach, you the player *are* the approach.

Once you know that you can handle a broad range of situations, playing matches means dipping into your accumulated knowledge for the appropriate response. In a match, it may seem like you're inventing shots for each encounter, but really, you're creatively combining solutions you've already developed in your practice. You stock this Resource Reservoir by hitting many balls correctly in practice; by facing opponents with a variety of game styles, and by analyzing your game objectively and then going out to hit more balls and do more analysis to fill in the gaps in your arsenal. You become *positive* as you become truly *prepared*. And when you are prepared and in full command of your abilities, you are positive. And later, confident. And maybe later, endorsed and photographed. In other words, who you are as an educated, skilled player is always with you. What you have to do to prepare for an important match is to *practice as you always do*.

In recent tennis history, there is no player who more exemplifies Coach Al's sports philosophy than Roger Federer. Federer's technical excellence makes him extremely hard to beat. He simply possesses more skills than anyone he plays. He is positive and confident because he knows that there is virtually no encounter that will drain his resource reservoir. Federer has a positive attitude and confidence because he is also better conditioned than the majority of his opponents. He succeeds because he's built his game on Coach Al's two pillars of non-sports-psychology sports philosophy; *conditioning* and *consistency*.

EAT. PLAY. LOVE.

Coach Al also observed that if you are running out of energy or your blood sugar dips, or you're just plain tired, all the stroke consistency in the world won't help you from losing focus. Once you do, your confidence begins to falter and you become negative. When this happens, matches you could have won slip away. How do you avoid this game enervating negativity? By being well-rested, well fed, fit and technically proficient. These pieces of preparation give you the best chance to be positive, confident and focused. These three attributes of all successful players are the results of extensive, productive practice, thoughtful preparation and obsessive, egotistical self-care. Take care of your strokes and your conditioning and the proper mental attitude will follow. Once you have assimilated the strokes and have the endurance to use them from start to finish in a match, your matchplay will inevitably improve.

Coach Al was not exactly saying that there is no sports psychology, but rather that those who peddle positive mental attitude as a technique *by itself* and those who claim that a frame of mind will make you better, mistake an effect for a cause. You don't get better because of something called "sports psychology." Instead, the better you technically and physically get, the more you possess an actual sports psychology that will work for you. Tennis may be 140% mental (more in some matches), but that mental edge is made possible by what you've done to prepare physically. Once you've put in the practice, make a plan to meet some opportunities and find some lucky results in the process. With that settled, let's focus on focus.

GAME TWO – DON'T LOOK NOW
(Constructive Distractions)

"Any occurrence requiring undivided attention will be accompanied by a compelling distraction."

Robert Bloch

Distractions. Distractions. Distractions. Our brains seem to need them, but they can sure get in our way. They arrive without invitation or warning and confuse us, misdirect us and veer us from our goals. It was ever so. Think of Odysseus, or Frodo or Anna Kournikova; larger-than-life characters pursuing great and noble quests, bushwhacked, sidetracked and brain-racked by unexpected temptations and unwanted complications; not to mention Calypso and Circe, Orcs and Enrique Inglesias.

DISTRACTED FROM DISTRACTION

Let's focus on the good news for a minute. Or, if that's too long, then a few quality seconds. You see, despite our fragmented, multi-tasking world, there are just two types of tennis court distractions: **Disruptive Distractions**; those truculent foes, oddball events and off-topic reveries that overturn our game plan throw us off our course; and **Constructive Distractions**; the replacement thoughts and habits that we develop to control and counteract them. Like fighting fire with better firepower, we can teach ourselves to redirect our mental wanderings and keep ourselves moving forward on our path. To quote T.S. Eliot, we need to be "distracted from distraction by distraction".

Now what was I saying? Oh yes, distractions. It was either Shakespeare, Hemmingway or Vic Braden who might have said, "Tennis players talk about wanting to be able to concentrate for a full match. Try concentrating for one game." Let's add, "Try concentrating for one whole *point*." You may be in top condition and you may be learning to approach each match with a calm, positive energy; yet things come up every once in a while, that just throw off your rhythm. Before the match or during; what do we do about distractions?

What we *should* do about match distractions is focus on the task at hand and ignore all that other brain activity. Very easy to say, but so is "live simply", "drive 65" and "eat your veggies." All good ideas, but like full focus in a tennis match, hard to actually pull off in real time when the result's on the line. And really, how interesting would life be if it were just steady incremental progress to ever more momentous goals? I don't know about life, but I think the game of tennis would *still* hold our attention. Assuming then that we don't need more mountains to climb in our chosen sport, what do we do about the diversions, musings, longings, goofy goings-on, strange vibes and odd externalities on the tennis court?

It's long been hypothesized by those who theorize, that a problem recognized is a problem half-solved. And if it's not half, it's at least a good 46 or 47%. So, in order to replace your disruptive distractions with constructive ones, you first have to identify what they are. Even this is not easy, and it too takes focus. Though there are infinite individual specifics, roughly speaking, disruptive distractions like any good eternal conflict sort into two basic groups: **Internal** and **External**.

Internal Distractions are the ones we bring with us to the match. You see, unlike me, *you* have a life outside of tennis; and though you enjoy playing, you find that you often come to the court thinking about some "challenges" from work or home or school. And no matter how much you want to play well and forget about them, these background thoughts keep vying for your attention. When your focus splits between distraction and action, the distraction lingers and the action suffers.

External Distractions are the ones you meet along the way. Even if you come to the court in a clear state of mind, ready to play, without a care in the world and with a bulging balance sheet (big "ifs", mind you) you may still find many disturbances abounding and a-bounding at you along the way. Here are a few destructive tennis match diversions grouped under the general heading –

How Can I Concentrate On The Match When My Opponent –
1. Looks angry?
2. Looks happy?
3. Doesn't call the score?
4. Calls the wrong score?
5. Calls the score too often?
6. Cheats?
7. Accuses you of cheating?
   Or even weirder,
8. Is too polite?
9. Makes ridiculously generous line calls?
10. Praises your bad shots that dribble in for winners?

11. Dresses funny?
12. Unknowingly makes silly faces?
13. *Knowingly* makes silly faces?
14. Hasn't kept up on personal hygiene?
15. *Knowingly* hasn't kept up on personal hygiene?
16. Is ahead in the score despite a total lack of talent?
17. Covets your racquet, clothes, shoes and date?

QUESTIONABLE FOCUS

All good questions. But even that's not all of it. In fact, it's just some of it. Because maybe it's not the opponent. Maybe it's other stuff. It's too windy. It's too sunny. It's too calm. It's too cloudy. The spectators, or the road nearby or those planes flying overhead are making too much noise and it's hard to concentrate. Or, it's too quiet. Or, it's alternately noisy *and* quiet and together the combination is driving me batty. Or just before I left the house / office / hotel room / Lamborghini garage, I had a fight with my wife / girlfriend / husband / boyfriend / teenager / boss / lawyer / investment advisor / Lamborghini mechanic. (Maybe the last one not so much. They're usually pretty nice. I've heard.)

If you've played tennis for very long, or a week, you've probably heard another player or yourself invoke one or more of these perennials, and most likely more than once. These complaints sound like excuses, but most of the time they're actually honest explanations for why it's so hard to play well in the real world. We may look down on players with weird excuses, but who among us doesn't have some?

Tennis is hard enough. Does the situation we play it in have to be hard too? Why can't we play tennis with only bland, businesslike opponents in perfect conditions? And, if there is a crowd, why can't it be abundant and enthusiastic, but respectful? And during play, shouldn't all ambient noise above 30 decibels stop and let our fragile, fleeting concentration be unbroken and absolute? And most of all, can't everyone in our lives just take a moment to seriously groc the *earth-stopping importance* of our chosen sport and restrain themselves from foisting *their needs* on us within a rigidly specified interval before any: match; important practice or other time we were hurrying off to hit a few balls?

All good questions. Or, at least, all *typical* questions. Much as it represents the height of inconsiderateness and rude interruption, in the actual physical world of real tennis matches, one or more of the elements above usually intrude in an attempt to derail us. So, what are we supposed to do? Follow the Epicureans.

The Epicureans? What does tennis concentration have to do with cooking? Nothing; and neither do the Epicureans exactly. You see, before they were re-branded as Foodies, the Epicureans were *the* name in Roman philosophy. Marcus "The General" Aurelius and his cohorts were not only warring, they were musing and writing. Not as much as the Greeks, but still a fair quantity of quite-relevant-to-the-twenty-first-century stuff. The Epicureans essentially believed that the events of this world we value as "good" or "bad", are not intrinsically good or bad at all. They are simply events. What matters then is not the event itself, *but our reaction to it.* Various new-age writers and "thinkers" believe they invented this idea. But, like the toga, the Roman candle and the WWE, the western version of this proto-psychological philosophical theory started in the Roman Empire. In tennis as in all sports, the most successful practitioners are the ones who are able to let in the flow of external events and then thrump their opponent anyway. On the tennis court as on the Roman battlefield, there are events and then there are our reactions to them. To once again invoke my mentor and erstwhile Epicurean philosopher, Coach Al, since the mind wants to react and since it can only take in positive images, it is important to give that mind something *positive and helpful to your tennis game* to focus on.

INTERNAL DISTRACTIONS

Internal Distractions are potentially the easiest to fix. Turning potential to actual. That's the rub. Here's one match play example. It's the opening game of a match against a numbingly steady baseline opponent. After struggling through a tedious, mid-paced, un-tactical twenty-three-and-a-half shot groundstroke rally, you begin to envision what a long day it's going to be. Playing this opponent looks like it will be difficult and un-fun because your groundies can sometimes go on the blink. The importance of this match running headlong into your questionable steadiness goes around in your head; mixed with the on-court realization that pusher baseline tennis doesn't hold the thrill for you it once did, if it ever did. However, to reach the later rounds and the better opponents, you've got to beat this one. Your mind also starts to stray to some undone tasks around the house and this toxic blend of dread and diversion takes over and you quickly lose a couple games. If your mind keeps straying away from the business of landing the tennis ball in the court and instead locks onto avoiding the difficult course ahead or leaps forward to some undone honey-dos, you may lose a match you could win. You need to replace your destructive thoughts with something constructive and give your active mind something psychologically nourishing to keep chewing on instead. You have identified the distraction and now you need one simple, constructive, helpful mantra to keep you on track and eliminate the distraction. What can you do? What would Nadal do? This doesn't happen to world-class athletes, does it?

Of course it does. But, great athletes are able to summon phenomenal focus to help them through. They can do this because they employ trainers, sports psychologists and swing coaches to help them incorporate great techniques to keep them aimed at their goal; and sometimes they just hate to lose. (A great focus inducer.) However, their minds, like ours, are beset by many of the same composure busters. What sets the pros apart is the tools they bring to the court. That and the car they drive, how many vacation houses they own and who they date. By throwing lots of cash and expertise at the issue, they have trained themselves to automatically employ techniques for dismissing their detracting thoughts as soon as they feel them arise. In fact, in the most finely tuned tennis players, minute mental adjustments are being made at all times during a competition. Thoughts like – bend my knees, keep breathing slowly, I think I'll buy the Bentley.

Sports commentator fawning and hyperbole to the contrary, no athlete in any sport is born a tunnel vision robot, able to proceed exclusively with the task at hand, never entertaining any competing thoughts. (Although it's hard to know that sometimes.) All athletes wrestle with the same demons and the same sirens. The question is: since your mind does this jumping around and since, in most cases, it *needs* to do this jumping around, what are we going to do about this need?

OFF-THE-SHELF TECHNIQUES FOR
STAYING IN YOUR GAME

No costly retinue required. These techniques are within everyone's grasp. As you develop your match play game, catalog *one idea* and *one back-up idea* per stroke that will bring you back to that stroke and help diffuse nerves and counter negativity. When things got tense or my mind wandered, these were some of my constructive distractions. (These may be a useful starting point. Or, like ironic facial hair and pencil jeans, they may not work for you at all. Feel free to develop your own.)

SERVE SCATTERINGS –
Watch the ball contact the strings. (Main thought).
Swing at one speed through the motion. (Back-up thought).

GROUNDSTROKE GLITCHES –
Quiet lower body/bend knees. (Main)
Follow through. (Back-up).

VOLLEY VARIANCES –
Early racquet position. (Main).
Racquet head at eye level. (Back-up).

My one thought gave me something to think about when I needed to make the shot in a tense or an adrenaline-filled occasion. This thought was easy to remember without any complex decision-making during a match. I found that simple, mechanical self-pointers kept me from going negative and reinforced correct technique.

ANOTHER MATCH PLAY EXAMPLE

Consider the "easy" put-away floater shot. Here's a no-brainer closing chance that should be a gimme winner, but is often a frustrating, teeth-gnashing point-losing error. For what should be for the better, but is often for the not-so-good, this set-up is found in singles and doubles at every level of the game. Your kind opponent unwillingly but providentially floats a medium-high no pace mishit to mid court. You see it, eyes wide and say to yourself, "I'm going to put this juice ball in the blender!" You salivate. Your pulse increases. Your mind whirs. You think, "This is an easy ball. I'm going to kill it." And with those thoughts, you relax your technique, over-amp your power, swing like a madman and blast the ball into the fence, and kill it. Using constructive distraction technique, there is another way.

This is how the revised version – Juiceball 2.0 – might go. You approach the sitter volley as calmly as the adrenaline filled match state will allow and call up your volley positive distraction. First you say to yourself, "Racquet head at eye level". Then you take in the location of the ball, lay your wrist back into its proper, elevated position, split step early and solidly, watch the ball make contact with the strings and put away the shot. These mechanical stroke thoughts allow you to exchange the idea of the **outcome** (crushing the ball for a winner) with the **cause** (correct volley technique and eyes on the string/ball contact) and gives you the outcome you want and much greater onlooker cred.

THE MATCH PLAN

Specific constructive stroke distractions work for strokes, but what about strategy? A more general constructive distraction that helps align your strategy is the **MATCH PLAN**. Like a racquet, a pair of shoes and a working knowledge of the scoring system, you need one for every match. It should be a very simple plan, like "hit to the opponent's backhand." Whatever it is, it should be only one thought. Then, whenever a strategic decision is called for, you simply go to your plan. This is possibly the best constructive distraction. By contrast, the typical thumbing-through of a vast brain-o-dex of possible attacks, counterattacks and subtle and intricate strategies is a perfect way to bring on indecision and paralyzing errors. Best to leave those particular pleasures for your opponent.

And, really, since tennis strategy is simple, keep it simple. Find out what the opponent doesn't want to do and make them do it *all the time*. Picking on an opponent's weak side is a time-tested way to score points on their errors. Rarely does more attention make a stroke better in match play. Usually, more use creates more mistakes. Starting by playing to their backhand usually pays off. If it doesn't, have a back-up plan for your match plan. Whatever you decide, be sure to use only one match plan at a time.

FORGET ABOUT THE SCORE

There are of course a raft of other pressures whose currents lead us down the river of mental haze. What do we do, for instance, about the mind straying from its task and wandering unproductively all over the mental landscape due to the tension and hopes and expectations of competition? What do we do about the pressure we feel when it's close to the end and we have a chance to win? What do we do about the big moments? Game point? Set point? Match point? How do we keep our focus and composure? Let me humbly suggest three ways—

Ignore the score.
Focus on mechanics.
Pursue the method, not the outcome.

You should of course always know what the score is. If you don't, you may have to count on your opponent and unfortunately opponents have been known to "forget" in their favor. So, *know the score*, but *play every point as though there were no score.* The harder you chase the goal of winning by watching the numbers, the farther away the win gets. You have only a certain amount of influence on the outcome anyway. Your opponent's play has a lot to do with the final score. And not just by miscalling it. If you focus on the score, you will inevitably be distracted by it and tighten up and play below your ability. If instead, you concentrate on what you can control – your stroke mechanics, your breathing, your attitude – you will have won even if you lose in score. Many times, I play practice points with my students, where we don't keep the score. We just play points to perfect the mechanics of playing points. In some of your practice match sessions, do the same. Have each server serve four or six points and then rotate servers. Be aware of how well you play, not how well you score. Then, make this approach a match habit.

CARRY-ON BAGGAGE

What about some of the other distractions I first mentioned? They need solutions too. A common problem for recreational players is **Life Distractions**. Life distractions are internal ones you bring with you like a toxic duffle bag to the court. I'm sure you know the feeling: sometimes life just takes over your life. You arrive at the court with a confused whirl of undone tasks and unsolved problems on your mind: The errand you need to run. The report you need to write. The choice between Mexico, Montana or Maui for ski week vacation? (I wish.) Though you have a match to play, your mind is not going to be on your tennis game. Instead your mind will be dividing its efforts 50/50 between your personal and business concerns and your tennis game – with the distractions taking both 50's.

What is the solution? Well, first and most importantly, once you get to the court, take a moment and be glad. *Be glad and be grateful,* because despite whatever else is going on in your life, you've *escaped* the intense gravitational pull of your everyday life and made it to the tennis court to *play*. So, whatever those personal tasks are and whatever business issues have your mind in a knot, snip them Gordian-like and turn your mind to your sport. Secondly, since you're here for exercise, health and enjoyment, don't sabotage those benefits to your personal well being with negative thoughts. And third, since one of the benefits of exercise is its ability to calm and focus the mind, let the act of playing tennis help you find a solution to the irresolvable conflict or unsolvable problem you dragged with you to the court; *after the match.* Here are three simple calm-affirming reminders for your on-court composure on a hectic day –

Hurry.
Try to catch your breath.
Rush on to the next thing.

Just kidding. You've already mastered those. Instead, try these —

Stop.
Breathe.
Take some time.

Creating a straightforward, three-step ritual like the one above (or doing even *one* of the three above) will help you realize and be fully aware that you're at the playing area and it is now time to *play*. You're not dealing with those problems from home or work right now. You are an athlete on a tennis court. And you are here to recreate; and maybe re-create yourself while you're at it. So stretch, breathe, tie your shoes again. Don't answer your phone. Put a new overwrap on your grip. Breathe again. Don't check your e-mail. Take a few slow-motion serve swings and loosen up a bit. And don't send that text! In other words, connect to the activity of tennis and *disconnect* from all those other, intrusive thoughts. Develop your own tennis phrase. It can be as simple as; "I am now a tennis player". Whatever it is, make it one repeated phrase that will bring you into the here and now.

What I'm suggesting may take some practice. (Duh) At first, like a well-coached volleyer recovering to the ready position, your mind will try to return to your carry-on life distraction(s) during the match. But stick with your simple phrase and simple thoughts, and you can remind your mind to use its formidable power to help you be a better warrior; not to be a better worrier. This discipline of un-entangling your intentions will help in many areas of your life. It is nice if the rituals you develop relate specifically to tennis, but a yoga breathing or meditation exercise will still serve the purpose. If all of this sounds difficult or ephemeral, don't turn off to the message. What we're really talking about is slowing down your actions and your breathing to create focus and relaxation. It will divide events B.T. (before tennis) and T.G.I. (the game itself) and help you focus on the task you're engaged in R.N. (*right now.*)

MATCH NERVES

Armed with some tools to help you participate fully (or at least, more) in the tennis match *you chose to play*, you may nevertheless feel nervous when you start. This can be very distracting. The golf pundit, David Feherty, once wrote that it wasn't necessarily a problem being nervous on the first tee, (for our purposes, hitting the first serve or playing the first point of a match) the problem was being nervous *about* being nervous. This meta-consciousness creates micro-nervousness which can feel like mega-nervousness.

It is normal to be exhilarated when you start a competition. You just can't let that exhilaration throw you off. Acknowledge this burst of hyper energy, and then don't fight it. Instead, learn to manage it. The great, thoughtful and conflicted champion, Andre Agassi, said that in order to relax in the first few games of a match he concentrated mostly on his breathing. That was, when he wasn't thinking about his issues with his father, his divorce from Brooke Shields or his toupee. (Those items did *not* help with relaxation.) I believe that Agassi's breathing insight can work for many players. Just try and avoid his other issues. Monitor your rate and depth of breathing and recognize that it may be alarmingly quick and shallow at the start of a match. Focus on slowing it down and deepening it. This will reduce your pulse rate and your nervousness. Develop a comfortable breathing rhythm and you will find your strokes settling down as well as your heart. And, by the way, your hair looks fine.

EXTERNAL DISTRACTIONS

Let's assume for the sake of hope, optimism and dreams coming true, that you *do* learn to calm yourself internally. This is a big victory. However, there are still those other *external* distractions to deal with. For instance, what about the opponent we mentioned earlier? The one with the annoying habits. Here's an answer you weren't expecting. To the extent that you can – and this will definitely take some (if not an unbelievable amount of) practice – **deny the existence of the opponent**. That's right; pretend that the opponent *does not exist*. This is not callous or as drastic as it sounds at first; although it's radical and challenging as simple solutions go. This means that while you are on the court, across the net, competing against this person, you are not a social being in a relationship with that other person. You are a tennis player trying to do what you need to do to concentrate on your own game and play effectively. And what you need to do is to resist the temptation to treat a tennis match like a bout of speed dating. You are not trying to make small talk and progress to more meaningful topics; you are trying to win more games than the person across the net from you.

Be fair and polite and give your opponent the benefit of the doubt; but realize that functionally, the individual on the other side of the net fulfills the same purpose as a malevolent ball machine that can actually serve. The opponent is simply a force to understand, analyze and conquer; not to swap stories with over drinks. (At least not yet.) That may well happen *after* the match and that is fine; especially if they're buying.

Besides good grooming, good manners and good form, you have one even larger goal in match play; *to try to win the match.* Win within the rules of tennis and be cordial and convivial and even friendly to the opponent before and after. But if you are to win, the opponent must be de-personalized during the match. The opponent is simply a fact. You hit more balls in the opposing asphalt more effectively than the fact does and you win. Don't, and the fact wins. You do not love the fact. You do not hate the fact. In fact, you don't feel any particular emotion. Why? Because the opponent is just a fact.

Easier said than done, however. Our social selves live by recognizing subtle facial cues, reading body language and making eye contact; especially in tense or combative situations. How can we look at the opponent as an objective obstacle if what we see when we look over the net is a smirking no talent, wearing weird mis-matched gym clothes and making bad line calls? It would certainly help if the opponent wore a mask (or a muzzle), or if you could see really well for only forty feet or so; but in practical terms, the best way to achieve this neutral state is to ignore the opponent's face, gestures and ridiculous expressions. They don't matter: nothing that the opponent does during the match besides hitting the ball, missing the ball or defaulting matters. Though the attitude and emotions of the opponent are perhaps the biggest distraction for most recreational players in match play, this distraction is potentially the easiest to solve. How? Stop looking at them!

Maintaining this type of match personality does not imply that you should become mean or aloof or haughty; traits that more than a few tennis players have been accused of over the centuries. And for good reason in many cases. Rise above this stereotype and just compete with, but don't engage with the other player. Ideally, you too are emotionally neutral about your own playing and only give yourself positive marks *internally* for what you do well. Outwardly (as Mr. Agassi once said), it's hardhat and lunch pail time. You are simply a person playing tennis, trying to do their best to play well.

By the way, none of these techniques should be used in rally-, lesson- or practice-tennis or on a first date *unless* you have alerted your hitting partner, instructor or prospective romantic partner that you want to work on your match attitude. (Even then, they're still not advised for the *first* date). Practice sessions are an ideal time for developing personal relationships with the other people on the court; and hopefully, very enjoyable times. Matches are enjoyable too; but they become enjoyable because of inward focus and the satisfaction that comes from the successful execution of your training and your plan. Matches *may* produce socially rewarding relationships after the match, but while the match is on, it's on!

I've suggested various techniques that have worked effectively for me, players I have worked with or players that I know and steal ideas from. And it is important to take in these two big ol' concepts—

1. **The mind (just like the body) wants to be at work during competition. And if you don't give it simple, positive ideas to work on, it will drift to potentially negative, distracting ideas.**

SO THEN –

2. **Give the mind something simple and positive to work on.**

Your focus may not be better yet, but you've sure read a lot about it. Here's what you should remember to help you. Acknowledge what gets in your way and your head during a match and resolve to replace your disruptive distractions with constructive ones. Experiment with different constructive distractions as you develop your ideal match method. After each match, identify points during the match that swerved you off your course and then figure out a simple, one idea constructive distraction that will give you a quick correction back on course. Take stock of how well you substituted useful thoughts for destructive ones. Ask yourself if you objectified the opponent. If it all went well, celebrate and write down how you did it. And if it's going to be a big celebration, write down how you did it *before* you celebrate. Taking a page from the scientific method, if it works once, you can make it work again and again. To again paraphrase John Wooden, "Plan for distractions and you won't be too distracted to plan".

GAME THREE –
THE NO'S NO

(Just Say No, No, No, No)

"There are always flowers for those who want to see them."

Henri Matisse

Few things in life are certain, but wiretap our house and you'll definitely hear three recurrent cants: "Is there money in that account?" "The dog did what?" and "No, no, no, no negativity." The first two are family staples everywhere and would probably be ignored. No, no, no, no negativity is a homemade nudge that won't balance the checkbook or clean up pooch indiscretions, but it works like a cranial whack to help right your attitude towards the dog, your personal finances and a passel of other preoccupations. When the national security apparatus investigates this expression, they'll keep it for the military. But in the interest of freedom of aphorism and better match results we're going to release it worldwide. Viral this!

Positive thinking and the "yes" are guru book fodder worldwide, but it's high time that negative negation joined the self-improvement movement. Renouncing the negative not only gives your life plans a kick in the conventions, it's vital in sports; especially in an individual sport like tennis where the player not only competes, but is also coach, linesperson, scorekeeper *and* cheering section. A convincing *nyet* to negativity clears your match-mind space and gives you room to say yes to all the things that will help your game. The first step onto the positive match outlook ladder is to acknowledge the negatives as they climb over your confidence and kick them off before they drag your game down.

NERVES AND SERVES

Maybe you've found yourself in this situation. You are serving, trailing four games to five, 15–40 in the deciding game of the deciding set of the tournament finals against your prime nemesis. You've just netted your big first serve and you are about to launch your less-than-fully-intimidating second serve. So here you are, down triple match, or more specifically, triple *championship* point to the player of all players you most want to beat. You get ready for your second serve and you body tenses. Objectively and logically, you know that you're not out of a tennis match until the score is final, and that it's always *arithmetically* possible to come back from whatever deficit you're in and win the match; almost any Serena Williams match is ample proof of this. But when you're actually in this situation, it's anything but objective and logical. You want to be positive, but your mind has other ideas.

What to do about the nervousness and emotions coursing through you in a tight spot like this one? Truly using your reasoned, analytic knowledge of the comeback possibilities when second-serving to save triple break point *could be* calming, productive and successful. And it *might well be* once you finish this chapter. However, what usually, really happens in these situations is the feeling that you're about to fall off a cliff; pulled down by a very heavy elbow. Instead of the light of reason coming to your rescue, the dark, insinuating minions of nervous doubt rise up to complicate your comeback. You don't see them. You may not even feel much different. But if you listen closely to your inner voices, you can hear their influence. Your inner antiphonal chorus incants – "I can't miss this serve. I can't double-fault or I'll lose the match. I can't miss. I can't miss." And you miss.

"I can't miss" may sound like you're getting rid of the negative, but chanting it like a mantra is not the way to do it. It's actually a great way to encourage it. Not only are you being hard on yourself; not only are you not living in the present, but most importantly you are *embracing* negative thoughts by letting them guide your brain and body. As Coach Al should have said a few chapters back, "The power of the negative when unintentionally affirmed this way is formidable." That is, when you repeat thoughts of things you are trying to avoid, you end up giving that avoidance thought positive power. Bummer. It seemed like such a good idea too.

Saying to yourself, "Don't mess up" is *not* an alternate way of saying "You can do it." The only similarity between them is *how the mind treats them*. Your brain uses each one of them as fuel to power your on-court actions. In other words, in a stressful situation like a sporting event, the mind puts all thoughts – positive *and* negative – to work without discriminating. That's why we have to carefully select the malt for this brew. Once you say, "I can't miss", your fight-or-flight focused brain fixes on the "miss" part and proceeds to obey that command. You sew the seeds of a negative outcome by making the avoidance thought the controlling thought. The doublefault you're dreading is just waiting to happen now and the nemesis across the net is just waiting to gloat; neither option is a good one.

MIND OBEDIENCE

Nervousness leads to negativity. So when you're in a tense match situation, acknowledge your negative thoughts. There is nothing wrong with you if you have them. (Except, of course, the big, glaring psychological stumbling block we're devoting a whole chapter to.) *Acknowledge them to get beyond them.* Detrimental thoughts naturally occur in pressure situations like our triple-grudge-match-point-scenario. Among other things, these thoughts shield us from disappointment. And here's why. Disappointment is really unpleasant when it surprises us, but isn't as bad when we expect it and prepare for it. Our mind (bless its heart) tries to lessen the blow of the letdown from the potential, impending loss by letting us say (to ourselves, at least), "I *knew* this was going to happen. I could have predicted it." Well, my friends, not only could you, but *did* you. And not only did you predict it; you *enabled* it by embracing and reinforcing and promoting the negative.

Tennis matches are rarely won on hope, but they're often lost on expectations. The way out of the second serve dilemma is simple – forget trying to coax the ball into not going out; *just hit it in.* As Coach Al was also fond of reminding us, "It's always fundamentals. And when it isn't, it's just basics. Simply hit the stroke you've practiced." So, before attempting that all-important second serve, assume the conclusion you want. Create your own reality. Easy to say, isn't it? Regrettably, to date, humans *and* tennis players have done a much better job creating negative realities than positive ones. That's why we need to actively dispel our negative thoughts; so we can get some skill and experience with creating positive realities for ourselves.

GOALED MIND

Since you inadvertently assumed a conclusion you *didn't* want before, now purposely picture one you *do* want. Say to yourself, "I see the ball going in the square. I see my serve going in." Then visualize the serve you are about to hit landing in a specific spot in the service square.

That's it. No technical swing thoughts . No stroke pointers. Nothing involving steps or analysis. They won't help. The fight-or-flight response that happens when we're in a tense or threatening situation, shuts down the brain's *higher* reasoning processes anyway, and excess information is rejected. But that's okay. You don't need higher reasoning, just *some* reasoning and a successful second serve.

Speaking of reasoning, notice that you're *not* saying to yourself, "I am now going to serve an ace. The match will turn around and I am going to win." That may happen. I hope that if you're in this situation it does. In fact, I hope that if *I'm* in this situation, it does. But those types of grand plans are as much illusions, and that type of thinking and projecting takes our mind just as much out of present time as the nerve inducing gloom of the negative. Instead, be specific about one near-term step toward the goal. In moments of tension, you just need one uncomplicated, unconscious physical action to keep you here, now. And that action will only happen by reinforcing what you want to do: not by trying to wave away what you don't want to do. Remember, positives focus you on the moment. Negatives take you out of it. Positives keep you at the task at hand. Negatives distract you in every way. You need to take the steps towards winning in order to win. And you need to take those steps one at a time.

Unless your opponent impetuously defaults or unexpectedly retires from the sport during your match, you are not going to win the match in question by hitting in this one serve anyway. While it is true that you can't win without making the serve and while it may also be the critical first step in your comeback, it is still only one, single shot. And that's all you need to focus on – one single shot. You don't need to somehow instantly win back all the points you trail by, you just need to win this one. This is another reason why positives work so well; like Depression-Era parents, they are economical, practical and simple.

Negatives, by contrast, are like Congress, profligate, impractical and serpentine. Remember –

Negatives confuse and obfuscate.
Positives clarify and simplify.
(And remember, avoid the verb, obfuscate.)

Negativity is a crutch; not the kind that props up the hobbled, but the kind that props up characteristics that are hobbling us. There's more to negativity and how it dismantles and paralyzes your game than just what it does to your stroke production. Negativity, like any hissy little Hydra, is many-headed, dangerous and can regenerate completely from any severed part. Let us count the ways.

NEGATIVITY IS

Recognizing all your mistakes in a match; bemoaning them, cursing them, enumerating them and thereby casting them in mental concrete.

(It's obvious when you hit an unsuccessful shot. You see it. Your opponent sees it. Is there really any real or imagined value in rehashing it on the court?)

Not praising yourself for the good shots you hit.
(Remember, you are the cheering section. If *you* don't spur you on to greater heights, chances are on one else will either.)

Assuming the conclusion of a match based on the opponent's reputation, or ranking or seeding. As Coach Al often reminded us, "Everyone can be beaten."
(In other words, play the match, not the player.)

Assuming bad stroke outcomes and telegraphing them to yourself by saying things like, "I can't serve", "I hope I don't have to hit my backhand" or "I hate to volley."
(Self-evident. Right?)

Using old tennis balls because, "I'm not good enough to play with the new ones."
(See: Set One, Game Six rant.)

Slumping body language. Hanging head. Drooping shoulders. Shuffling gait. (Bad posture previews bad outcomes and lack of dates afterwards.) And those are just a few.

IT ALSO IS

Letting the game score or the set score or how you're striking the ball when you start a match determine your outlook. I once coached a junior tournament player who would step onto the court, hit two warm-up strokes (literally) and say "I'm playing terrible today!" Needless to say, much of our work together was about attitude, forbearance and the definition of "today". Besides, it doesn't matter how you start, it matters how you finish. In a tennis match, you can lose more points *and* *games* than you win and still win the match. If you start slowly, you start slowly. Everyone has their own, internal warm-up clock. Mine was frozen in some alternate time-continuum. When I played competitively, I would typically lose in two sets or win in three. Not invariably, but often. I didn't like this trend. I did all I could to change it, but there it was: my trend. I was a very slow starter. I realized this and worked hard to become a better player, and I didn't fight it. Indirectly, it taught me patience, a certain detachment from worrying about the outcome and the value of extensive pre-match warm-up sessions. It also led to my enduring interest in conditioning and concentration, since I was typically destined to play long matches. I went with it (after a while), didn't fret too much (after a while) and planned to play better as the match went on (always).

Start slow or start fast, but if you have a day where you and your technique are not on speaking terms, play hard and sweat but don't sweat it, and find some needy element of your game to minister to. It could be holding the grip with lighter pressure, breathing to calm yourself, perfecting some element of footwork or watching the ball make contact with the strings. Then even on a tortured day, you'll make some progress in some area. And, unless you're hustling an opponent for big money, don't excuse your game before, during or after a match where you didn't play to your standard. You don't need to prove to anyone that you could have or should have played better. Take your medicine graciously, then go home and make a list of ways you can improve. Then return with a better game and compensate for the last loss with the next win. Playing well is the ultimate rebuttal, after all.

RANGER ON

Even on a bad day, find good things about what you did. In Roger Federer's press conference after his unexpected loss to Tomas Berdych in the 2010 Wimbledon quarterfinals, Federer said he was disappointed to play the way he did, but followed that up by saying that making the quarterfinals was a good result and that many players would die to make the Wimbledon quarterfinals. He was not trying to convince the interviewer. He was reminding himself that despite playing below his standard, he was going to take a positive from the match. That's what champions do; they accentuate the positive and cheer themselves on, occasionally watching their own highlight DVD's. Most of that advice goes for the rest of us too. Find something positive to take from every match and have a friend make a highlight DVD for those times when you need some reminding.

You certainly don't want to delude yourself into believing you have skills you don't have and end up living in a fantasy world; unless, of course, you convince everyone else you know to live there too. You want to have a truthful, accurate sense of your game. You want to know what you can do and what you can't do, and then play the match with skill, gusto and abandon. You may not have the strokes you ideally want (who does?), but if you concede the match before you play, why play at all? As Andy Roddick said when asked about his mental outlook after losing the spectacular 2009 Wimbledon final to Roger Federer, "What's the alternative? You go on. You keep going." Andy's right. That's the alternative. In tennis. In life.

Plus, giving the opponent an advantage based on your self-perceived weaknesses or their peer-promoted reputation makes things much too easy for them. They have doubts and distractions of their own. Let them find their own solutions for them. And who knows? Maybe today isn't *their* day. Don't help them over the finish line if they can't do it themselves. Don't let *your* attitude win *their* points for them. Do play hard and give yourself every positive mental advantage. Keep in mind, even the strongest game has weaknesses; you are not the only player with a stroke flaw here and there. Admitting a gap or two in your arsenal is no reason to give up or feel sheepish about your chances. Instead, concentrate on what you do *well* and feel bullish (or whatever the opposite of sheepish is. Wolfish(?)) about that. Anyway, don't let your opponent win because of your self-doubts. If you stress what you do well, you will raise your game. If you stress what you *don't* do well, you will raise your opponent's game *and score*. Especially if you don't happen to be a world-class athlete with masterful strokes, give yourself another type of advantage – be *mentally strong*.

This is the preferred plan of positive action as it *should* work. And if you do really replace your negative thoughts and self-talk with positive thoughts and self-talk, it *will* work. But as with many things, quieting your manic mind during a match is not quite that easy. At first, your negative thoughts will want to stay and are hard to push away; even when you recognize them and deal with them and start to replace them. Just as in learning a new stroke or a new strategy, you will need to condition yourself to this new way of responding to these pressure situations and learn how to use a new technique to overcome an old habit. With positive thoughts comes relaxation. Calm allows you access to your practice game strokes and easy confidence in difficult match situations. Even if you're only slightly more calm, you can begin to execute technically-correct strokes in high-stakes, technique upsetting situations; *or* at least sometimes hit the shot you actually intended when you get a little rattled. Banish the negatives and replace them with positives and you will play better. A positive mind won't be protecting you from failure, but will instead open you up to success. The happy ending to this process is that you will win more points and then more games and sets and then more matches. And soon, the nemesis will seek lesser nemeses as you advance beyond the rivalry. All of which brings us to the other chiseled stone in the match attitude edifice, destined to land in the coach's aphorism hall of fame –

"PLAY TO WIN. DON'T PLAY NOT TO LOSE."

Playing To Win means approaching every shot intending to use correct technique to win the point. Play *your* game and don't succumb to your nerves and alter your stroke mechanics to try to be safer than the other player. Step into the ball; hit through the serve with a full motion (even on second serves) and try to do, in a match, all the things that make you effective in practice. Playing to win does *not* mean playing with your focus on the score, before, during or after the match.

Obsessing over the point/game/set tally is a good way to take your mind out of the match, tighten you up as you try to force the result you want and push that result away from you. Play each point and the score will take care of itself.

Playing Not To Lose means playing to try to avoid errors. Playing the score is one of the possible traps, but there are others. When you play not to lose, you play timidly and tentatively; not stepping in to your groundstrokes and guiding them in, tapping or short-arming the serve for safety, engaging in negative thinking and just plain not hitting in a game like you do in practice. Just as negative thoughts spiral in all different directions, (thus, I guess, becoming a shape other than a spiral) so too does negative technique. If, for instance, you start altering your forehand groundstroke by shortening it or ignoring your weight transfer, you have to invent adjustments and compensations and then more adjustments and compensations on top of those earlier ones. Life is full of enough un-intended consequences. Don't create any more. Positive, play-to-win technique simplifies your game, allowing you to hit the shots you have practiced; not inventing shots as you go in a tight match. Negative, play-not-to-lose technique complicates your game; forcing you to make corrections you can't concoct quickly enough for strokes you've never worked on.

Playing To Win also involves a realistic estimate of your opponent; best summed up as, *don't underestimate your opponent; don't overestimate your opponent.* See the opponent's strengths and weaknesses as they are, not as they initially seem. And then play against the true opponent, not the one as seen by your first impressions. An example–

An opponent might have a huge first serve that looks scary until you really begin to see that it only goes in only about 15% of the time. In reality then, this serve is not a terror, it's an error. On the other hand, an opponent might have an unorthodox, slow, side-spun backhand that appears weak. (You've *seen* this stroke.) However, when studied critically, you realize that this suspect stroke keeps finding the corners of your court and the opponent rarely misses with it. This stroke which looks like a liability is in reality a strength and something you should avoid whenever possible when playing this person.

Don't underestimate. Don't overestimate. Emotion and attitude aside, this is what we're really talking about. Use your brain. Play competitively. Play within your game. Play to win and keep in mind what *you* do well. You're not conceited if you do. Every player does many things well. To compete confidently and successfully, you need to find your strengths and build your physical and mental game around them.

These two big ideas – playing to win and saying yes to the positive – go together very well. Like salt water and taffy, high octane and gasoline, pretensions and contemporary literature, they are mixed because they match. Positive attitude allows good technique. Good technique creates positive attitude. And, as with any important project, the best time to begin to use these ideas, no matter on how small a scale, is *now*.

HERE ARE SOME POSSIBLE WAYS TO START

The next time you play a match, identify two or three negative thoughts and try to replace them with positive thoughts. If you find this hard to do when you're actually playing, that's to be expected. If it were easy, you would already have corrected your match attitude, dispatched a cadre of combatents and skipped this whole chapter. But since you haven't and you didn't, this is how you start to mature your mental game. In addition to adding some positive thinking, practice some sample visualizations off-court to answer some typical situations on court. For instance, find some memorable, one-idea course corrections for: pressure-filled second serves, game-ending floater volleys and even serve returns for a crucial break. Grooving your ball toss technique, improving your fitness and adopting some focusing tics like string straightening are other helpful game-enhancers you can practice anywhere.

The next time you play after this first time, recognize a few more negative thoughts and replace them with more positive thoughts. Substitute positive game-improving prompts for more subtle negative self-cues like bad posture, disparaging self-talk and early match stroke performance doubts. Your score may not immediately improve, but please don't worry, right now we're all about process.

The time after that, *play to win*. Dress like you mean it. Re-string your racquet. Arrive at the court early. Warm up. Hit some extra serves. Spend a few quiet minutes beforehand envisioning yourself playing exactly the way you want to be playing. Then, stand up straight, head high and play the whole match using the strokes you've practiced in the way that you've visualized. Your strokes may be wild at first and your results may be mixed. It may be difficult and you may backslide, but stay the plan and you will gradually find yourself hitting your practice shots in the match and scoring points with them. This will increase the more times you do it. You may progress, then regress – at least as far as the score. But, stay with it, this is difficult stuff. You are not only changing habits, you are reprogramming anthropology and biology; not to mention some pretty significant self-image assumptions.

Once you begin to consistently hit your actual strokes in a match, you've turned an important corner. From then on, add to these totals each time you play. After a few sessions of observing your inner workings and perfecting your outer workings, you will begin to change your game and you will come consistently closer to bringing your loose, intuitive practice game to the match court. This does not mean that all nervousness will be gone and that all negative thoughts have vanished; it does mean that you will be able to use a lot more of what you know you can do when it really counts.

And so, here's the final score – don't be negative in overt ways – self-thought and self-talk; and don't be negative in veiled ways. Don't court the negative in your life or in your tennis game. And keep in mind that even with the right attitude and lots of practice, this new approach will only really become part of your game when you've used it in a real match and beaten (or had a significantly better result than usual against) an opponent who previously had your number.

Back at home, the dog may still be on the NSA Watchlist for check kiting and those other preoccupations may threaten to thwart your progress, but know that they can't compete when you have an attitude to handle anything on court or off. When the mind is sold on the ideas of positive, play-to-win tennis you can truly say **no, no, no, no to negativity** –

And yes, yes, yes, yes to positivity.

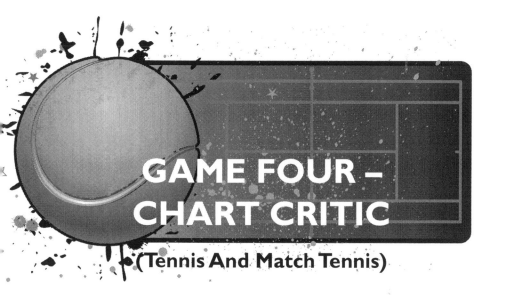

GAME FOUR – CHART CRITIC
(Tennis And Match Tennis)

"The more I practice, the luckier I get."

Gary Player

A man in tennis clothes paces on a Manhattan street corner. He button-holes a passerby, "Excuse me, how do you get to the US Open?" After a moment, Passerby, "Is this a joke?" Tennis Player, "In *this* book?" Passerby, "Yeah, sorry. Take the #7 Subway line and the LIRR Train. Get off at Flushing Meadows." Tennis Player, "Thanks, pal." Passerby, "Happy to help. By the way, name's Pete and I've been there myself a few times. That train's the easy way to go. If you *really* want to get there, that's a little harder and you've got some deciding to do." Tennis Player, "Deciding? What do you mean?" Pete, "My car's here. Gotta go."

BIG DECISIONS

Who was that guy? What deciding was he talking about? And what about a ride? Well, whoever he is and whatever the story is with that car, he's right; there is some deciding to do. Whether you want to go to the US Open, the USTA Sectionals or the next challenge court at the club, getting there involves some decisions: three of them, to be exact. First you have to decide to *compete*. Next you have to decide to *win*. And third, you need to decide that you're going to *learn how to win, and unlearn how to lose*. (Which is really one decision with two parts. So maybe it's not *exactly* exact.) The point is – winning's hard, but losing's easy. Sure, it may hurt right after, it may be embarrassing and you may not like it very much, but still it's remarkably easy to do. Most players can't avoid it at first. And it can easily become a habit. There's no conflict or controversy and opponents are more than gracious in letting you follow that straight, endless route.

But if you want to win, you need to set some new coordinates and follow a tougher course. You see, the road to winning isn't straight and easy: it twists and turns, frustrates and surprises. Following it takes steely navigation, alertness and stamina. And there's plenty to consider. You have the technical factors like your skill level and conditioning and your opponent's skill and conditioning. There's your own competitiveness and personality. And then there's this basic gut-level question: do you have the pure, competitive drive necessary to preserver through hardships, endure disappointments and commit yourself daily, weekly and monthly to improving your match game and actually beating other players when it counts? And of course there's this: do you really want to win more than you want to lose? If you answer 'no' to either or both of the last two questions, that's fine. Just practice, play some matches, let the score tally where it may and read this chapter for the craft and penmanship. But if you want to try to win, read on, because there's a lot that goes into it; a whole lot more than goes into losing. Here goes.

THE FIRST THING YOU NEED IS PRACTICE

Some of it you're doing and some of it you might have considered, but not started doing yet. And some of it, you had no idea you needed to do. Well, you need to do all of it. Correctly. We know that winning matches takes a winning frame of mind, and *practice* is the way to a winning attitude. But *how* should we practice? *How much* should we practice? And, *what* should we practice? If practice doesn't necessarily make perfect, does perfect practice make a perfect tennis player? As we said with sports psychology, it depends.

Let's split step back a minute and begin with a basic truth. Most tennis players love to practice. Practice ground strokes. Practice serves. Practice some volleys and some overheads. And that's a positive sign. But here's another truth – *just practicing strokes won't win matches*. Good strokes make your game look good, but there's much more to winning matches than great strokes. As many successful playing pros and their terribly flawed and incomplete games show, bad strokes are no guarantee of bad outcomes.

However, playing pros are excellent role models for other, perhaps more important parts of the match game. In the areas of competitive drive, perseverance and making the most of what you have, ***you do want to play like the pros***. Playing Pros cordon off their match life from their outside life, control their on-court environment and manage themselves and their emotions in a match. They get really good at it too. Because when they do, they win and when they don't, they lose. The reason why so many mis-taught, poorly-coached, basics-deficient athletes make a pretty nice living at a very complex sport is simply this: ***They know how to win matches***. As Arnold Palmer famously said, "There's golf and then there's tournament golf". To paraphrase Mr. Palmer, "There's tennis and then there's match tennis." And success depends on preparation, attitude and fortitude; and some on strokes. But not so much.

WE PLAY *BOTH* KINDS OF TENNIS

Instantly taking issue with our own re-working of Arnie's insight, there are actually **three kinds of tennis**: *rally tennis; lesson tennis **and** match tennis*. And if you want to win matches, you must pursue all three. *Rally Tennis* is typically the most practiced and the most enjoyable. Smooth groundstrokes yielded up by a willing partner; each player trying to create conditions to help the other player hit successfully and enjoyably. No serves. No transition shots. No points. No scoring. No pressure. No bad feelings. Just great hitting. *Lesson Tennis* builds skills. You pay to take the court with a concerned, consistent professional whose goal is to make you better through drills and exercises in a safe and supportive environment. Usually you get better.

Both rally tennis and lesson tennis are indispensable in creating consistent, reliable strokes. Still, as many of my students will attest, it's not always easy keeping these three categories of tennis separate. Players often confuse rally tennis and match tennis. Two players go for a friendly hit, but one of them keeps putting the ball away because "I can't get rid of my competitive instincts". More likely that player isn't consistent enough to rally and need an excuse for their wild shots and unplanned angles. Just as likely, players find themselves in a match unwillingly rallying the ball back to the other player when they should be putting it away. Sometimes, just as irrelevantly, players fault the lesson format for not being" *realistic*" (that is, for lacking the competitive intensity of a match), thereby missing the express purpose of a *lesson*. The instructor's goal is not to try to beat you, but instead to make you a better player so that other players won't. Not to mention the hidden difficulties of credibly creating match-like mis-hits and inconsistencies in a lesson. There *are* obvious uses for point play practice in lessons, but they need to be carefully constructed and explained. There is rarely any good that can come from making your instructor your opponent. However, there's always immense good that can come from making your opponent your opponent.

Each type of tennis has its place, but on their own, rally tennis and lesson tennis have only limited influence on vanquishing an opponent. *Only match practice does that.* But it's a decidedly different beast. **Match Tennis** takes the skills you learn in your lessons and the consistency you develop by rallying and whirls them in a blender knocking around in a tornado. (And other windy metaphors.) All of this is further complicated by the foe across the net trying to make it even stormier; often inadvertently making it also more unsettling and irregular. You need to have your strokes battened down and carefully moored if you hope to survive, outshine and still serve up a competent concoction. Even if you're hitting a lot of balls and taking a lot of lessons, you probably won't be able to weather the stroke squall. In fact, if you want to succeed in match play and you're not playing matches, you're only doing about *half* of what is needed. Perfect practice is perfect for certain things, but *complete practice* works better.

At least once a month (and sometimes every lesson) of every century I've been teaching tennis, I ask my students how they're doing in their various leagues and matches and tournaments. Often I'll get, "My game is never as successful there as it is here (on the practice/lesson court)". As a follow-up, I'll ask them how much they practice point play outside of their actual matches and they usually say "not much". Sometimes they say "never". It's not that I haven't promoted the idea, but like a teacher with second semester Seniors, there's only so much homework I can give. Those two answers (and the actual actions behind the answers) are the first things that need to change if any player wants to play matches more successfully.

MATCH TENNIS

Match tennis is different than rally tennis. Like table tennis and setting a table, it's essentially a separate activity. You need to train specifically for it, and know what to expect from it. In match tennis your opponent is *not* a hitting partner, and where there was no score before, there's now a score that counts and unfortunately no matter how beautiful your strokes look, there are no judges giving out style points. Any responsible teaching pro wants to teach the best, most efficient technique possible, but match tennis success comes from learning how to score points and defeat opponents with the tactics *each match demands*. You may like to hit deep, but if your opponent's weakness is the short ball, you adjust your strategy and play to that opponent's weakness.

In a match, there are some high-quality sustained rallies and some beautiful reciprocal shot-making, but that is only because neither side has made a mistake or produced a winner. Be clear about this – your opponent may be polite and cordial and, we hope, fair; *but on the court that person does **not** have your best interests at heart*. Though you are using the same strokes as in rally tennis, nothing could be more antithetical to rally tennis than this. The opponent wants to win more points than you and win them as quickly as possible, put the ball away or force you to make a mistake. Move you to one side and hit it decisively to the other side. Hit it deep when you're short. Hit it short when you're deep. Or just plain smash the ball and put it away.

And so do you.

But you probably know this already. If you've played matches at all, you're well aware of the stakes and some of the difficulties. Good. So what are you doing *specifically* to make your match play *better*? You and your pro can run drills for placement, transition shots and movement and for counteracting extreme pace, but I've not yet seen a lesson format that can duplicate the intensity, the raggedness of shots, the unpredictability of responses and the strange spins and trajectories produced by mishits that are not only part, but often the *bulk* of match play. (So, yes, in this sense the well-hit, well-placed, well-paced shots of a lesson are *unrealistic*.) Until you *repeatedly* face opponents who are trying to beat you and until you begin to know what types of shots to expect and execute in tight situations and until you've had to confront the looming and often terrifying possibility of *winning* and the nervousness *that* creates, *and* make shots to finally close out a match, you won't truly know what shots you can count on and what shots you need to improve to develop a winning game.

EVEN WINNING SHOTS MAY NOT WIN THE DAY

There is so much more to administer in a real, live match. First and forehand most, there is this opposing player who wants to beat you, and the energy and attitude coming at you is different from a hitting session or even a practice match. It's not anger, it's not malice, it's not pique, it's a volatile mixture of all of these things (malangique?) wrapped in an unusual nervous, aggressiveness. Part of solving the matchplay puzzle is figuring out how to handle this energy. Besides this opponent energy-dynamic, there are a bunch of details that aren't even part of lesson tennis or rally tennis that can occasionally become the focus of match tennis and can always make the difference between a win and a loss. For tragic example, I've seen many quite skilled junior *and* adult players lose points, games, sets and matches in tournaments simply because they didn't keep track of the score. The moral being that if you're going to lose, lose to the other person's superior talent, not to your own inferior attentiveness.

Here's A Partial List Of Match-Specific Details
That Make A Difference–

Keeping score, calling lines and switching ends of the court.

Handling fatigue, monitoring food needs, hydration, and depletion of energy.

Learning to keep the court order – where the balls are, what's happening around you, what your personal state is.

Gauging your swing speed for new balls and the way they behave. (Are you playing practice matches with new balls? You should be.)

Proceeding despite weird or bad court conditions and distractions like spectators nearby, traffic noise or a baseball or soccer game on an adjacent field.

Dealing with wind or sun or dirt on the court; or balls rolling across from other courts.

Blocking out distracting behavior or distractingly good-looking spectators or attractive players on the adjacent courts.

Blocking out opponent histrionics or diversionary tactics.

And Notes Of A More Personal Nature –

Managing the nervous energy that can over-adrenalize you when you step on the court for a match.

Avoiding the edgy, aggressive behavior you're likely to lapse into after confrontations over score and line calls and rules.

Finding your ideal match tempo. Do you play fast? Do you play slow? And how do you get back on tempo if you lose it or slow it down if it gets away from you?

Recovering when things start to unravel.

Losing or winning graciously.

And most important, coming back from a deficit to win, playing from a lead and closing out a match for the win.

Come up with solutions for all those things, and you still face the gnarliest obstacle to pulling it all together to win a match – besides a cheating opponent, terrible weather conditions or a large, lunchtime burrito – *you can't stop in the middle of a match to figure these things out.* As with other facets of this exquisite and complex sport, these skills need to be worked *on* and worked *at* in practice matches and then in real matches so you sort through all these details *before* you arrive at the court. In other words, you need to practice confronting the randomness and requirements of match tennis in real time in the real world. It's impossible to say exactly how much of this experience is enough. It varies by player. Even if you play matches often, it can take some time – often a few years – before you've seen and dealt with enough match particulars to really face adversity and complication and still stay on your game. Not to mention that some players have a much higher tolerance for losing and so let it go on too long despite having learned how to control the courtkeeping details.

Most players never reach the level they'd like to; primarily because they don't play enough and partially because of the thoughtless way they play when they do play. At some point, to really improve, you have to play an unbelievable amount of tennis – for recreational players that might mean playing four hours every day for a month, *with specific goals and exercises* – in order to make sustainable, irreversible progress. That sounds daunting; and it is. Most of us will never be able to do it, but fortunately, it isn't an all-or-nothing deal. According to a popular theory, expertise takes 10,000 hours of practice. But for the record, even that amount can't be just any old kind of practice. Practicing the wrong strokes for that long will make you either: very good at them; a playing pro or a tennis parent. As much as a many-thousand-hour, intensive, structured program would help any player, committing to even *some more* practice, done thoughtfully and consistently will produce measurable results; measurable, *positive* results, no less. Here's a less-than-10,000-hour way to make some headway on some irreversible progress.

A ROUTINE MATCH ROUTINE

Let's say you could play four days a week, (I know that's a boatload of tennis for most of us, but just sail with it for now) here's how you should use that amount of practice time. One day should be a *lesson*. (I *would* say that.) One day should be a *hitting session with a hitting partner*, where you can practice correctly executing your strokes. On the other two days – or 50% of your practice time– you should play match tennis: *one practice match against a good quality opponent* and *one real match that counts*. The ideal opponent for these practice matches is a player with a different style game from yours whom you can beat about half the time and who beats you about half the time. The ideal opponent for real matches is someone highly ranked or at least highly regarded that you can mercilessly clobber and reduce to tears; or, at least post a respectable score against and have a laugh with afterwards. Admittedly, four days a week is a big commitment. So, if you can only practice three days, cut out one of the match days. If it's only two days, get a new job *or* alternate the lesson and practice day one week with the lesson and match day the next. Then begin aggressively investing, job hunting or finding a financial backer so you can get the count up to four.

At the recreational level, few players divvy up their time like this. In fact, few players even think of "divvy up" and "time" in the same tennis sentence. Players play hard, but not always smart; with the result that most players spend a lot of time and effort perfecting individual, isolated parts of their games – usually the ones that don't need much work anyway – and then step onto the match court and find that the match situation is novel and terrifying. Out on court, they get nervous, their strokes regress and their game shrivels; they get flustered by the unexpected and the unfair, and all because they simply don't play enough matches. These players are happy and comfortable rallying or at their lesson, but they freeze up when facing an actual opponent; and it may take them almost the whole match to thaw out. By that time, it's usually too late. The match situation needs to become *routine*. It needs to be *a* routine. If it becomes ritualized and familiar, you can step onto the match court relaxed, ready, adrenalized, yet comfortable.

Once match play is routine, it can become instinctual. Responding on instinct makes you a better match player. Instead of strategizing a response for each shot, the split second decisions and shot choices you make get conditioned by responding to lots of shots hit by a lot of opponents in a lot of different situations. Those are the lots of a match player. Information is stored in your brain's match computer and pulled up quickly in actual match situations. The more matches you play, the more complex shot combinations and responses will be natural to your game and integrated.

HOW'S THAT EXACTLY?

Okay, picture yourself in the middle of an energetic singles point. (Yes, that *is* you I'm talking to.) You hit a forehand down the line to your opponent's backhand; he/she responds with a deep crosscourt backhand, which you barely reach and hit down the line without much pace to his/her forehand. You're now out of position and their follow-up salvo is a deep, pace-full forehand rocketed to the very back of your forehand corner. A winner, right? Not necessarily. It depends what's in your match brain. If you've played quite a few matches and seen this set-up a few dozen hundred times, you probably have an intuitive feel for where that salvo's headed. So as soon as you loft your down-the-line backhand opponentwards, you burn some expensive proprietary rubber for the forehand corner; reach their predictable projectile and crush it back even harder. (Yes, that's the future you doing the crushing.) Your match-developed intuition told you to move early. So you pursued their shot with a plan in mind and won the point. That's how it could work and with match practice, it can. Really.

To be intuitive about stroke combinations takes many hours of practice and real match play. If it didn't, then everyone could do it *intuitively* intuitively. But it does and that's why they can't. Matchplay practice hours also make you intuitive about the offensive combinations *you* will use against your opponent. Serving wide to a right-hander's backhand in the add court often forces a weak return to your "T". When it does, simply put the ball away to their forehand corner. This tactical instinct becomes second – or third to third-and-a-quarter – nature to persons who play a passel of points. And you want as many of these limited-brainer points like this as you can get. Not to short change on-the-court tactical reasoning, but you would prefer automatic, no-deliberation winners whenever possible. In real matches, most points aren't neat and tidy, what with *both* sides improvising, scrambling and reacting; not to mention tired, hungry, sore and dealing with the numbing assortment of other match details previously enumerated. So, take order, predictability and automatic, unconscious winners where you can find them, and then use them for all they're worth.

PAYING OFF THE TITLE

It has either been established by now (or else you *are* just reading for craft and penmanship) that just hitting strokes won't win matches. But then there's this – *just playing matches won't necessarily win matches either*. Yes, you will become more relaxed, able to handle erratic events on court and your practice stroking will show up more often; but relaxation, looseness and familiarity *only set the stage* for better match play. The next step is to know your tendencies and find out which strokes or combinations of strokes you rock and which you schlock. This brings us to: **Charting**.

Complete practice regimens involve match play. Learning from that match play involves **data**. And data comes from **charting**. Once you're playing more practice matches, you need to know your strengths and weaknesses in *numbers* and *percentages*. The best way to acquire this important information is to **chart your matches**. Here's a sample chart from the Pre-Federerian (also known as the Hewettozoic) era; but it will give you the idea.

OCCAM'S RACQUET

THE AFOREMENTIONED CHART

Date: Time:

Tournament:

	Forehand	Backhand	Approach	Lob	1/2 Volley
Unforced					
Forced					
Winners					
	FH Volley	BH Volley	Overhead		
Unforced					
Forced					
Winners					
	1st Serves	% In	Dbl Fault	Aces	Winners
Player					
Opponent					

Game Score:	1	2	3	4	5	6	7	8	9	10

Player: Round:

Score:

Opponent:

Comments:

(By the way, if manual charting by pen and paper isn't your style, there are now some very smart smart-phone apps that make it as easy as a first round bye.)

The *idea* of charting is simple, remembering your shot percentages in the middle of a hard-fought match isn't. Tennis memory is selective. It is difficult to be analytical about your game while simultaneously *playing* your game. It would take Jedi mind tricks to play a point with full focus and analyze the point with *any* focus; much less play games or sets and keep track of statistical strengths and weaknesses with any accuracy. But if you have a willing (or coerced) accomplice who will write chart or enter smart phone, you're on your way to feeling the full joy and benefits of tennis statistical analysis. Charting will tell you how many winners, forced and unforced errors you had in your match in each set in each stroke category. It will show you your first serve and second serve percentage by set and game. It will highlight where you scored points and where points slipped away. It will reveal what you're actually doing compared to what you think you're doing.

DATA SETS

I often chart my junior students' tournament matches. After the match I generally do not confront them with the chart data immediately; and not only for fear of reprisal. The chart numbers can be sensitive, in-flammatory information; and if not inflammatory, sometimes depress-ing or as they say, annoyatating. Usually, we review the match chart after the match emotions have subsided: some hours later or even the next day. *Exactly when* depends in part on the height of the win, the depth of the loss and the emotional composition of the player. As a rule, the only kind of question I might ask directly after a match – and the most important one from a positive sports frame-of-mind perspec-tive – is, "what did you do *well* today?"

One post-match session brought a revealing answer to my question. I had just watched a junior player we'll call Boris – not his real name; name of a famous German serve-and-volley guy – play a match *he won*. In this match, his chart showed that he had hit four blistering, paint-removing, high-velocity forehand groundstroke winners, *and* – <u>twenty-six unforced forehand errors</u>. These forehands were mostly long, though a few went into the net. His answer that day? "I hit my forehand great!" He remembered the four atomic forehand winners and the win itself. Lost in the pleasant glow of these winners and the victory were the twenty-six forehands that gave his opponent *twenty-six free points*. (Remember, we're looking for 70% success or more on our strokes. His percentage that day was 13.3%. And his steady serving, not his forehand was the stroke that carried him.) We didn't discuss it any more that day, but the tennis science sure was talking to me. I am pretty certain that Boris went home from that match thinking, "My forehand is an awesome weapon!" And I am certain I was thinking, "We have really got to improve his forehand percentages."

Boris was right psychologically to focus on the positive and there's no doubt that we would eventually build his offensive game around this explosive stroke. But the numbers from the chart were a good, useful counterpoint to his forehand optimism. They told us what shot to work on in order eliminate a big group of unforced errors that could be fatal in a closer contest. There's much lip service given these days to the platitude "you only learn from your mistakes" and charting would seem to support this cliché, but does it? It certainly provides the opportunity to recognize errors, but I think it may have at least equal value in chronicling success. Coach Al was not only fond of talking, he was fond of saying, "You only learn from what you do *well*. What you learn from your mistakes is what areas you need to improve." In other words, knowing where you fell down is not the same thing as getting up. As far as improving your game, *only repetitive practice of correct technique and correct habits will make you better.* And mistakes? Identify them and avoid them: *they don't make you better, they make you **aware**.* So, remember, play to your strengths, practice improving your weaknesses and don't take any wooden shibboleths.

THE BEST PLAYER THAT DAY

There are two types of typical tennis-playing humans: those who remember the spectacular moments and ignore the errors, and those who remember all the errors and blot out the successes. In some cases, it's the same human. In the cases where it isn't, any objective measure of stroke success would help both of them. Charting hips you to your percentages for *all* your strokes. It's valuable information; even, and maybe especially, for the strokes you are scoring with. Not only will it reveal where the errors are, it illuminates your winning percentages too.

Do it a while and charting will become part of the match routine; like calling the score before you serve, initiating all on court decisions and developing a special, but *almost* imperceptibly different inflection for saying "my ad". Find your strengths and build on them. Find your weaknesses and improve them. Then make all four of your practice days, you-get-better days. On lesson days, review the chart and do technical work on problem areas. On practice days, practice your improved technique and then bring it to the court on match day. And once you return to the match court, chart away!

Not all match tennis is won by the best player; and in some cases, the match winner is simply the best match player *that day*. To be that player and get the best long-term results (i.e. wins) on many different days, you need to be skillful, competitive, focused, adaptable, resilient and analytic *on the court*; not to mention courteous, kind, obedient, cheerful, thrifty. brave, clean and reverent off of it. Some of these traits may be natural; others may be learned; still others may be imposed on a player by good coaching or their scout leader. All of them need to be practiced. To adapt the famous and almost always mis-attributed quotation by Friedrich Nietzsche, "What doesn't permanently discourage us, makes us stronger." Extreme adversity won't hurt us if we are accustomed to it. Fortify your game to stand up to the competitive and sometimes random onslaught of influences from the opponent, our surroundings and ourselves; and thereby, win.

Complete practice makes for perfect practice. Complete match players are match winners. Like the tennis player standing on the New York street corner, who asks: "How do you get to the U.S. Open?" There is another way – practice. Complete practice.

GAME FIVE –
DON'T GO CHANGIN'

(Be The Player You Are)

"To your road, you just don't doubt it."

Earth, Wind and Fire ("Getaway")

As Yoda might say, "far we have come." And know it don't you, right he is. Practice what you've read so far and the tangibles of tennis are now within your grasp. But the *in*tangibles; just like overweight relatives at the holidays, those are a little harder to get your arms around. You see, now that the technical work is done, spiritual quest we are on. It's time to ask two big, potentially game-changing questions that go to the heart and soul of why you play this game: *Does your game reflect you?* And *have you found your tennis Doppelbanger?* The answers to these two questions will complement and complete the simple, intelligent, well-dressed game you've been fashioning. It only makes Occam's Racquet sense that the simplest way to be the best player you can be, is to be the player you *should* be. But who is that? And what is a *Doppelbanger?*

Have you ever watched a player on television or at a tournament and said to yourself, "That's how *I* want to play tennis!" Of course you have. We all have. This is how the pros get started. This is how a personal style begins. This is how some players end up with racquets that look great on TV and discombobulate their strokes. You see your dream style and you instantly know exactly how you want to play. Not only do you want to play that way, you want to play that way *now*. Quivering with excitement, you head to the court to learn how to transform yourself into the player you now know you were meant to be. Yet, when you go back for your next lesson and tell your tennis pro about the player you'd like to emulate, your instructor laughs politely (or, in some cases, derisively) and says something like "wouldn't we *all?*" And with that slice of rhetoric left hanging like a short, high lob, your dream deflates, your enthusiasm flags and your quivering congeals. You resume your steady force-fed diet of groundstroke and serve repetitions; the stated or unstated goal being your incarnation, in this life, as a high-percentage, hug the baseline, clear the net and avoid the volley defensive tennis machine; by all means, not the aggressive, slashing and blasting maestro you channeled on Tennis Channel. And you promptly list your new stick on Ebay.

WHAT IS THE MEANING OF LIFE?

More importantly, what is the point of tennis? If playing the game that called to you from deep inside the Billie Jean King National Tennis Center isn't, what is? Is the goal to create meaning though consistent groundstrokes that clear the net by nine feet while retrieving every ball, putting it back into play and hoping that your opponent drowns in a flood of unforced errors? Is defense really the name of *your* game? Are you actually, deep down, the conservative player your instructor wants you to be? *Or*, are you a stroke-walloping, charge-and-sort-it-out-as-you-go, caution-and-percentage-be-darned, multi-hyphenated sonic-sphere-smacker? Or something in between? Hmm? While you're pondering that, consider this classic syllogism –

GAME FIVE – DON'T GO CHANGIN'

Tennis is a sport.
All sports are supposed to be fun.

Therefore, tennis is *all* sports.
(Wait…)

Therefore, tennis is supposed to be *fun*.
(That's it.)

The reasons you play tennis are simple: recreation, health and *fun*. Of the three, the most important and enjoyable is *fun*. A loss is only truly a loss if you lose your perspective. The worst day playing tennis beats the best day (insert verb for any other activity here) any day. And after all, what is a win worth if you're not playing the game the way you want anyway? Okay, maybe some adulation, a league championship or a couple million dollars *depending*; but what is it *really* worth if it doesn't speak to your soul? Life is too short and too long and too much exactly the length it's supposed to be to play tennis for anyone else and their idea of how you should be playing. Construct a game that speaks to your innermost tennis muse and pleases *you*. You are after all the one putting in the hits, the sweat and the dollars. Get the game you want. Hit the shots you want.

I work with a player who I believe will eventually choose to develop a dynamic, hard-charging offensive game. So far though, we have been working hard on her stroke production and consistency to build her match confidence and we haven't focused much on the power side of her developing game. This is typical. But recently she told me, "I have to confess something. Sometimes I just want to hit the *felt* out of the ball!" (And maybe she didn't exactly say, "felt") Anyway, far from being mad or upset as she thought I would be, I thought she had a great idea and a great insight. She was beginning to glimpse her playing personality and wanted to test it out a little. I encouraged her to hit some big felt but to just know what may happen and not to get discouraged if that felt-relieved ball flies long.

This is but one example. I work with other players who are very polite to the ball, wanting it to retain as much felt as possible for as long as possible. There's no need for them to become baseline bashers, a steady hit and retrieve game will meet their needs and their goals.

YOU, YOUR DOPPELBANGER AND YOU

The point is this: every player at every level has a playing identity; a core "court self" that tells them who they are on the court and speaks to the style of game they want to play. In "real" life, a Doppelganger is your alter ego. Your on-court self then is your "Tennis Doppel*banger*": your tennis alter ego. All successful match players have one. Some players love to retrieve and return, happy to wear an opponent down and win points through repetition and consistency. Other players love to play offense; approaching the net on a short ball, or after a serve or after a return, then moving to the net to put the ball away. Still other players are happiest blending these various stylistic elements. But *every* player needs to identify their Doppelbanger and decide what it really wants to do. When you play a match, you don't just want to hit the ball, you want to hit the ball *somewhere*. Similarly, you don't just want to use strategic elements willy-nilly, higgledy-piggledy and in no apparent order, you want strategies that support, reinforce, enhance and further your style of play; a style that should be deeply suited to your on-court personality. And that's what you need to figure out; though it's not always obvious.

Your Doppelbanger may or may not match your off-court personality. Some people are aggressive, risk-taking, type "A" personalities in their off-court life, but play an in-control, low risk, high percentage retrieving game on court. Some are conservative, even tempered and measured off-court and are aggressive offensive players on court. You might just be the actuary who is a wild serve and volleyer or the smokejumper who plays defensive, middle-of-the-court safety tennis. Some people go into community theatre to explore hidden or forbidden layers of their personality; you may want to explore an unaccustomed facet of your character on the court. There's nothing wrong with tennis as role-playing, tennis as therapy or tennis as frustration expulsion. It's cheaper than psychiatry.

Speaking of which, I played briefly at a club where a local judge was a member. On the tennis court he was not at all the reasoned, deliberative personality he was in the court court, but instead a hard-serving, high-risk, all offense serve-and-volley specialist, who lived and died by the big shot and the grand put-away and slam-and-blast coup de grace. In his case, his Doppelbanger was either a manifestation of an under examined corner of his personality that couldn't come out at his day job; *or* the tennis ball was a convenient, ethically neutral stand-in for some of the defendants (and lawyers) he faced that day. Or maybe both. For him tennis was exercise *and* therapy. No matter why you're there, to play the best tennis you can, you need to find your type. Here are the options –

A MENU OF PLAYING STYLES

Undecided – (Everyone at the beginning; Some Pros on an off day and Many Recreational Players)
Does a little bit of everything but without a plan.

Defensive Baseliner – (Some Pros and Many Juniors and Adult League Players)
Returns the ball from every nook and cranny of the court, hoping for a profusion of opponent errors.
(Early Nadal. Caroline Wozniacki.)

Offensive Baseliner – (Many Pro and Amateur Players)

Controls the tempo and angles with blistering groundstrokes winners from the baseline. Uncomfortable spending much time in the forecourt.

(Later Nadal. Robin Soderling. Kim Clijsters. Most others on both tours.)

All-Court Opportunist – (Some Pro and Amateur Players)

Plays baseline defense or offense until a short ball or other inspiration presents a net-rushing opportunity. Typically also uses finesse shots like lobs, off-pace groundstrokes and dropshots.

(Radek Stepanek. Martina Hingis. Engaged once, incidentally.)

Serve and Volley – (Almost No Pro and Not Enough Amateur Players)

Volleys behind first and some second serves; may even chip and charge on returns.

(Taylor Dent. Amelie Mauresmo. Hardly any others)

Many players switch playing styles as their games develop. It's common after the undecided stage, to start out as a defensive baseliner and then decide if that is your game or not. Many players never think to move beyond this stage. But as with many things in life, you will have the most success and peace of mind and fulfillment if you choose one road; your decision-making flowing from a big concept that guides you. Not only will you be consistent in your decision-making, you will decide quicker and more easily. Starting without a big idea and then trying to play a consistent style would be like trying to pick a political candidate while holding no political philosophy – what do you mean, doesn't *everyone* do it that way? – you would end up changing your mind with each new campaign promise, because you have no framework and no set of beliefs to compare each idea against.

(Incidentally, I don't in any way want to trivialize match tennis by comparing it to *politics*, but the root issue – consistent choices based on values – is similar. And luckily, all the choices in tennis are good ones.)

WHO AM I? WHAT DO I WANT?

These are the questions that determine education and career decisions, relationship choices and engine displacement. So, in tennis, a clear idea of your "court self" tells you how to practice and what to work on to become the player you see yourself as. What you want to get out of your tennis game can be an important guide in determining not only the type of game you will play, but also what you should concentrate on in your lessons. Make sure your lesson give your game some room to grow and change.

If your twenty-first century game doesn't speak to you, then what was the purpose of the 60's, the 70's, Existentialism, Existence Preceding Essence and Individualism? Hmm? Why pursue an *individual* sport if you follow a groupthink approach to it? Ask yourself, "how would Camus play?" Don't check your individualism and personal expression at the tennis court gate, let loose your Doppelbanger on the court. Say to your pro, "There are more things in heaven and earth, pal, than are dreamt of in your little play-like-the-pros philosophy." Or words to that effect. Be the player you want to be. In fact: *go ahead and play like the pros if you want to*; just don't do it only because it's the latest pre-fab fad. The annals of history (and not just *tennis* history) are papered with plenty of really bad ideas that were the latest craze at the time. Play the game you play because it expresses the player you *need* to be. And by all means, while finding a game that speaks to your deepest strokegeist, let your pro in on your dream, and if they want to help, let them. Maybe they'll learn something.

STYLE COUNSEL

By the way, it's important to note that style is *not* synonymous with talent. Everyone has a style inside them, but not everyone is a talented tennis player inside. Everyone can *learn* to play tennis, but the idea of perfect, innate ability lurking deep in everyone, needing merely to be released to be realized is a misleading dash of false hope. It's a charming fiction, but in decades of teaching, I've worked with some great athletes with impressive hand-eye skills, but I've never met a *natural tennis player*. First, because tennis is an *un*natural game and second because tennis is so little about athleticism, speed or strength and so much about physics, engineering and the mechanics of stroke skills, and these skills need to be taught, not intuited. Style is another matter. Once a player has learned the technical side of the game, they will find a particular style of game inside of them waiting to be expressed.

Great players find their playing style and then build a game around it. In fact, this is a big part of how they become great players. Patrick Rafter the charismatic Australian champion of the late 1990's loved the offense created by coming to the net. He didn't seem to care much for long rallies. Lleyton Hewitt, another prominent Aussie winner, loves the long rally and the battle of strength and endurance that defensive baseline tennis produces and is not as comfortable approaching the net. Both men have won Grand Slams. Both have been ranked #1 in the world. Both approach the game differently, having each found the style they are comfortable with.

What you *want* to do is often determined by what you physically *can* do. The player *you* want to emulate may have different strengths than you. You may love the way Rafael Nadal tirelessly chases balls and you may love his very physical style of tennis, but if you're not fit enough to pull it off, you will want to increase *your* fitness or dial down your dreams. Be Nadal within your physical capabilities. Don't lose the dream, just edit it a little bit.

Maybe Nadal isn't your idol. Maybe Stefan Edberg is. Maybe you want to be a serve and volleyer. And after your instructor's huge initial dose of derision and negativity, you decide to try to work with his or her usual background amount of derision and negativity and make the best of it and learn to serve and volley. You try some serve and volley exercises and discover that the aggressive forward movement, the stopping, starting and split-stepping and the prospect of being passed or hit at by your opponent's serve return or groundstrokes makes you uncomfortable. You may still want to play an aggressive game, but decide that instead of serve and volley that you will look for short ball opportunities to come to the net and volley. To make this work, you will choose short balls that allow you to hit deep approach shots: shots that don't allow the other player the chance to pass you, and give the best chance to approach the net and avoid being passed or attacked. In this way, even though you've accepted the idea of offensive tennis, you've customized the idea to your style of play and personality.

IF THE STUDENT HASN'T TAUGHT

While the foundations of any advanced tennis game are the same; extensive, complete practice, wads of cash spent on lessons and a very indulgent spouse, significant doubles partner or family; ideally, an experienced, advanced player should be able to execute a shot *from any area of the tennis court*. Therefore, proper, comprehensive instruction should focus on building consistent, dependable all-court skills. Once those skills have grown some roots, it is then time to figure out what skills you want to *emphasize*. This may take some experimentation.

Find an instructor who doesn't just teach *strokes*, but instead teaches the *game* you want to play. To assess how effectively you will work with this person, (and the following advice is directed to intermediate and advanced players) consider this: in your first few lessons, work on a variety of strokes; try various playing approaches and then, based on what you like to do, ask the instructor for their impression of what type of playing personality you have. If what they say matches what you feel, you have a good fit. If they are unable to articulate what they see as your tennis persona, if they really don't get the sense of your question or if they simply revert to some pre-ordained orthodoxy, ask them what makes them characterize your game they way they have. Discuss it and entertain the possibility that they may have seen something important in your game that you haven't. (This *may* sometimes happen) But after some give and take, if what they say is antithetical, inimical or just plain opposed to what you really want to do, consider searching for another instructor. Remember, tennis is part of your joy – make sure you enjoy it. Let your Doppelbanger play!

PROCESS THIS

Getting in touch with your Doppelbanger is by its nature an ongoing, never-finished work-in-progress. On any particular day for any particular match, you come to the court with whatever game you have *at that time*. If you're still working out components of your serve and volley game, don't debut it in a match. Make sure you've ironed out the glitches in some practice matches before asking it to be sleek and wrinkle free in a match that counts. The pressure and distractions inherent in matchplay can upset the delicate, deliberate calibration natural to new skills and make them difficult to execute. (Translation: when you get nervous, you hit weird.) When hard-to-perform meets match pressure and produces low percentage, you may come away feeling that the new skill isn't working, and that it will never work. But, most likely, that new skill simply needs more time and practice to properly integrate into your arsenal.

Once you do introduce a new skill (such as aggressive volleying) into your game repertoire, instead of expecting unqualified success, give yourself a simple, numerical goal for each match. Your goal can be, "I will approach the net 15 times today." That means that no matter what the outcome, you are successful and have reached that day's goal merely by coming to the net 15 times. Miss them all or make them all, just by coming in, you've met your goal. Increase the goal number in successive matches to a final target number. Once you've reached this numerical target, it is then and only then that you should begin to look into your percentages and start to assess your progress.

Tennis, like golf, martial arts, piano and risotto-making requires consistent, conscientious practice, dedication and wrist strength. It is a high-skill sport that can take a lifetime to master. As such, progress can seem slow. Take a deep breath; mastery takes time. There are really no easy successes or epiphanies in tennis. (If there were, there wouldn't be so many instructors.) There is steady, rewarding progress and satisfying long-term results and improved health and waistline.

The final satisfaction comes from developing the type of game you want to play and then learning, practicing and perfecting the skills necessary to play that game. When you can act intuitively, knowing that you have the chops to respond to most every strategic situation in your chosen style, you will be the player you were meant to be.

GAME SIX– IMAGINE IF YOU WILL

(The Game For Intelligent Life)

"When I was 40, my doctor advised me that a man in his 40's shouldn't play tennis. I heeded his advice carefully and could hardly wait until I reached 50 to start again."

Hugo Black

The closing game of this second set is not about physical or mental instruction, it's about perks, spiffs and add-ons. And not just one-time, blink and they'll disappear special offers either. What tennis offers is good for life. Spectacular promotions, popular trends and exercise fads come and go. Our sport is here to stay. So sign up now, it's a great deal. Tennis offers value-added benefits as soon as you begin and doesn't buzzkill you with any hidden fees, tricks or blackout dates. It's a virtuous circle rewards program, available anytime to anyone who wants to join; 365 days a year, going strong for over *ten centuries*. No restrictions apply. It's a stimulus package that really works.

In a nation that's slowing down, spreading out and composting brain cells; a nation grown heavy, sluggish and dim by lack of movement and over-pitched on quick fix, no-staying-power exercise programs, and almost instantly mini-storaged get-in-shape contraptions, tennis is an efficient, elegant and multi-faceted solution. It's not only great exercise and a competitive challenge, but in most climates in most seasons, it gets you outdoors in earth's very own G-2 type main sequence star and tanning facility, the sun. You can be competent in a few months, but it's intricate and varied enough to challenge you and delight you for your whole life. And it's *not* golf. Tennis is the other lifetime sport – the one that *relaxes* you. Of course, you can ignore all the benefits and simply pursue it because it's stroke ripping, sweat dripping, VS-gut-and-Luxilon-hybrid-string-job-shredding fun for the whole family. It'll make you look good and feel good; it's a wholly wholesome pleasure.

PERSONAL TIME

You may take up tennis for one of many reasons: it looks great to watch the pros on TV; my spouse / boyfriend / girlfriend plays and I want to play with him / her; I need exercise and I hate running / cycling / the gym, etc. and I need the game element of tennis to distract me from the workout part; I like the outfits / racquets / shoes / lifestyle, or, I want to hit the ball really hard. That's some of it. Beyond all of that, maybe the hard-edged, beautiful esthetic of the game grabs you; the sun beating down particpantward, the crisp geometry of the court, the solid, fluent, smoothness of a clean ball strike or the adrenaline rushing at you, clearing your head and bouncing your step. Or maybe it's a particular moment: the knuckle-bumping, bro-hugging camaraderie of a great hitting session; the teary-eyed frustration of the vanquished foe; the scorching winner that sealed the second set. It could be the beauty and contradiction of the sport; the manners, civility and decorum; mingling effortlessly and comfortably with furious action, raw emotion and violent, repetitive asymmetry. Or maybe you just like to hit the ball really hard.

Then there are the intangibles; the bigger, loftier motivations. Tennis can appeal to the heroic and the talented in us. Watching the pros may inspire you to emulate them. Great champions have ignited tennis passions in many countries and set the course of many fiery young athletes. Maybe it's done the same for you. Or maybe the game has put you on a path to personal improvement by learning and improving at a difficult, rewarding skill. No matter whether you reach your ideal game, go on tour or rally with friends, you just can't avoid being fitter and healthier than when you started. When all is hit and done, you're in for a treat because tennis has other unintended consequences: what Adam Smith – if he'd played tennis – might have called "The Invisible Forehand." You may start out playing tennis for your body, but end up with a buffed brain in the bargain.

VIRTUE BY ASSOCIATION

The sport's dual lures have snared a world-class assortment of historical and current possessors of buffed bodies and buffed brains (sometimes both) – Henry VIII, Napoleon, John Locke and Bode Miller. Dustin Hoffman, Robert Plant, John F. Kennedy, Wallace Stegner, Gerald Ford and Lindsey Vonn; John Paul Stevens, Teddy Roosevelt, Vladimir Nabokov, Mike Wallace and Mathew Perry; Ludwig von Mises, John Maynard Keynes, A.A. Milne, Ronald Reagan, Herbert Hoover, FDR, Regis Philbin, Jack Nicklaus and Shannon Elizabeth. And no wonder the game attracts such a following of successful, often important personages. As Robin Williams observed, "It's like chess at 90 miles per hour."

Even at 60 or 70 mph, tennis places high demands on the whole athlete: the full-body physicality of basketball or volleyball; the masterly technique of golf or fencing; the endurance of distance running, the hand-eye sharpness of hockey or baseball and the mental acuity of bridge or chess. And it's not easy. If it were, it would be racquetball; and we all know what happened there. It's difficult and it's complicated. And that's a good thing. To interest you for your whole life, it has to be.

Tennis' pervasive subtlety and illusive proficiency guarantee its difficulty. Even impressive bodies bearing great athletic gifts can't always bring it under their powerful sway. Being big and strong and fast is not enough. (Although it doesn't hurt. Occasionally, it even helps.) Tennis also requires exceptional balance and agility; not to mention quick reactions and adaptive, dynamic movement. Sometimes it favors power, but it always rewards control and control of that power. Some very talented athletes have come to tennis with the idea of quickly mastering it based on their success in other athletic fields. And they often find, to their amazement, that it is not the Muffy-and-Biff-sipping-Mint-Juleps-pulses-barely-stirred-after-a-social-doubles-drubbing-at-the-club they thought it was. Some stay for the long term and become proficient, some get frustrated and move to other athletic pursuits, or poker. But tennis welcomes everyone, and will always welcome you back from your dalliances, no questions asked, whatever your ability, age or interest. All it asks in return is your dedication, understanding and patience.

And patience is a tennis virtue. Since a complete tennis game requires proficiency in as many as twelve different strokes: serve; return; overhead; all the variations of groundstrokes; volleys; half-volleys and drop shots, the skill demands make it impossible to learn quickly. Some cognitive scientists claim that it takes a mature, coordinated adult ten thousand repetitions to learn a new, complex skill, such as a forehand. (I wouldn't know. It took me easily 10,003 or 10,004 if I remember correctly.) To build a comprehensive quiver of talents, you are looking at more than one hundred thousand repetitions; and many thousands more to perfect it. In fact, there's an old saying – "I don't fear the person with 10,000 skills, I fear the person who has practiced one skill 10,000 times." Me too. Now, think about someone with 10,000 skills practiced 10,000 times. Wow. And yet that's sort of the story of tennis. Not quite in those quantities maybe, but daunting still. Even if you hit one thousand balls per week under an instructor's care, you are still looking at almost two years of training to build the *basic strokes*. When you add to that stroke combinations and transitions and the ability to hit from different positions on the court, it becomes clear that even at the raw numbers level, tennis takes a long time to learn. That, and many cans of balls, a forward contract for replacement grips and a long position in sun block default swaps.

LIFE'S WORK

Then there are the responsibilities the game throws at you. Since you don't have a team to support you (at least not in singles tennis unless it's WTT, Davis Cup or Fed Cup), you *are* the team. You need to know all the shots, all the strategies and scout all the opponents. To ensure the fluid functioning of your twelve strokes all over the court in different positions and set-ups, against many different types of shots, capabilities and strategies, you need to compete against a broad and mixed ability quilt of opponents. Even just in rallying, tennis differs from just about all sports, because the flow of play is only as smooth as the person you're hitting with. Your opponent can determine by their game what type of game you can play. This means, faced with inconsistency, you need to be very consistent. You need to stroke really well when your opponent isn't. This takes more practice and hours and repetitions; balls, grips and sun block, and a steady stream of unsteady, idioscincratic adversaries.

Factor in all of these variables and you can see that it can take a lifetime to master the game. In fact, maybe "master" is a too strong a word.

You get very good at it and very good working with it, but it is the rare day when everything is humming the same tune at the same time. The skills, the physicality, the strategy, all are in a continual balancing and re-balancing flux. You have to have strokes to execute a strategy, but conceiving of and attempting a strategy will tell you what strokes you need. And sometimes just clearing the net is the day's challenge. The intense demands of getting your game pointed in a direction, steering it through obstacles and keeping it on course will distract you, focus you and never bore you; yet there are other tangible rewards besides strokes, strategy and excitement that literally make the game a lifesaver.

BODY OF EVIDENCE

It's an efficient full-body aerobic and anaerobic workout. It is potentially inexpensive and it is egalitarian. Since the scoring system makes it a meritocracy, you don't need a pedigree or a coach's or committee's hand-choosing; you just need to win to succeed. And if you don't want to compete, that's fine too. For the competitive, it's like non-contact boxing: violent, asymmetrical, but basically safe. For others, it's a family sport and a couples' sport. Either way, just by playing you get serotonin, Vitamin D and increased bone density. Without intending to, you can end up fit, relaxed and really tan; and feeling younger.

As John Ratey of Harvard Medical School says at the beginning of his talk on sports and the brain (quoting philosopher, Neal Young); explaining why you want to keep exercising as you age, "It's better to wear out than to rust." Meaning, use your body up. Do something with it and for it every day you're alive. And why not tennis? It ages quite well. Many tennis players still play in their 70's, 80's and 90's. Tennis magazine recently profiled a man, 97, who plays every day against a teaching pro friend at 11:00 am. He was asked why and he said, "What else am I going to do? If I stay home, I just fall asleep." He's onto more than a little something. Now and as we age, we can go to sleep or we can go forth and go for it. Tennis gives us a way to exercise at a fitness-, talent- and age-appropriate pace. We will not only age gracefully, but also hit a nice down-the-line backhand while we're at it. And that is just how it helps the body. The brain benefits too; now and as you age.

BIG MAN ON HIPPOCAMPUS

Tennis helps you intellectually. It takes intellect to play the game and since the better you play, the more you think, playing more makes you more intelligent. It's a bountiful, cranial circle. It teaches you how to construct your own game and how to handle and out-strategize new and known opponents, literally while you're on the run. It can take wit, humor and guile to adapt our bodies as our capabilities change. Tennis helps you figure out how, by forcing us to creatively alter our games as we get stronger or weaker, faster or slower, obliging us to develop new strokes to meet new physical and mental challenges. It's also a social game, one filled with interaction, meaning and decisions. Just like life, it engages you at every level and never stops testing your invention, or your ingenuity.

The brain itself gets ripped and golden too. Recent research in the medical and psychiatric fields (particularly the work and writings of our psychiatrist, tennis player friend, Dr. John Ratey) has shown that a consistent program of aerobic exercise not only helps combat obesity in children and adults, but more importantly improves brain mass and brain functioning. Going for a run or playing a set of tennis before a test or a big meeting will make you mentally sharper. Dr. Ratey singles out (pardonable pun) tennis as one of the best activities for providing exercise, mental stimulation and an environment of play – all necessary to promoting brain functioning in adults – and as an ideal activity for adults over 50 to help reverse the brain's deterioration by up to 15 years. So it's okay to occasionally watch mindless TV and chill on the couch with no personal improvement on your agenda; just make sure you get in some court time too.

The benefits of tennis are not limited to adults. Children who participate in a regular exercise program (ideally 45 minutes per day, five days a week) have much less tendency towards obesity. They also study more effectively, test better and have fewer discipline problems. Dr Ratey, who has published multiple books dealing with ADHD also points out how exercise promotes growth of the front part of the brain: the area concerned with impulse control, anger management, focus and time management. Tennis can be a lifeline for ADHD children as well as helping to control depression in both children and adults.

THE FINAL POINT

Those are the simple, smart facts of tennis. Live simply. Live smart. Play often. Play smart. Have fun and, by all means, treat yourself to a daily mind/body/soul workout. So, the final lesson in our final instructional set is this: though our focus has been on game improvement and match proficiency, the array of skills you strive after and collect on the tennis court combine to make you more than you were when you started this game. Tennis is a wonderful blending of an on-going process leading to an ever-improving product: you. A game that is a rare combination of physical skills and mental skills. A game in which working smart and playing smart are halves of a great whole. A game for the intelligent life of intelligent life.

WE'RE NOT DONE YET

(The Aftermatch)

"All the theory in the world won't lift up one cup of coffee."

A College Professor (Whose Name I've Forgotten)

To attempt is to do. To achieve is to do. To improve is to do. Reading about tennis helps change your mind, and you've now done *a lot* or reading, but to really change your game there is still one after-match task you need to go out and *do*. And it's a big, all-encompassing doozy. Here it is. The next time you go to the court, visualize that you will –

HIT EVERY BALL IN.

Now this is undoubtedly *not* the final bit of instruction you'll ever receive; but as you weave all the many bits together, it's the final piece you'll really *need*. And it is certainly the final and missing piece for the players we watched on that August day.

OCCAM'S RACQUET

HIT EVERY BALL IN.

Yes, I'm serious. I know it sounds ambitious or misguided or a little crazy (or a combination of the three), but try it. This one thought will change your game. (It would've changed theirs.)

HIT EVERY BALL IN.

Imagine it. I dare you. Do it. I double-break-point-down-in-the-third-set-final-game dare you. This is our destination. This is our culmination. We've cut through the complicated clutter of conventional court concepts and this is the final string that completes Occam's Racquet.

HIT EVERY BALL IN.

It sounds impossible, but really, it just takes some application. Consensus of the governed, accurate weather forecasts, a universal rudeness cure; those are impossible. Hitting every tennis ball in the court is *not* impossible, it just takes some time and effort. And time. Nothing in physics contradicts it. Probability and statistics might doubt it, but what do they know? They've never played tennis. And we've already mentioned how well they do on the weather front. (So to speak.)

HIT EVERY BALL IN.

It's possible. The tennis court is 36' x 78'; that's a big area. It's possible. If you have simple, repeatable strokes, it's possible. If you hit up the middle of the court with some margin, it's possible. If you stay positive, it's possible. This isn't just about *not* making unforced errors. It's about hitting every defensive, offensive and maintenance shot *in*. *And it's possible.*

In fact, I know a guy who says he knew a guy who met this guy, and you know the rest. I'm sure it's been done somewhere. One of my students recently told me that it was her goal. She came up with it. I didn't. She thinks it's possible.

HIT EVERY BALL IN.

How? Start small; the same way she is. Hit one ball in, then two, then three. Next, hit in every ball for one point, then one game, then one set, then one match. Long practice rallies will help. Thousands of proper practice shots will help. Good technique and concentration will help. Believing you can do it will *really* help.

HIT EVERY BALL IN.

Here's the great part: it's actually not about being perfect. If you get close to the goal, you've made huge strides – in technique and concentration and attitude. And played a game-changing amount of tennis. It's about pursuing an ideal, regardless of the outcome. It's day-to-day motivation for the court and the pursuit is never-ending. Like yoga, it isn't about doing it flawlessly; it's about doing it.

HIT EVERY BALL IN.

You'll be asking a lot of your game. But you now you have the skills and the outlook. Even if your strategy is to hit winners at every opportunity from every part of the court, those winners still have to go *in*. To win points, even off opponent errors, shots still have to go in. In fact, hitting *any* ball in the court begins with imagining it is going in. And take a moment and ask yourself, what is the alternative anyway? Imagining it *won't* go in?

HIT EVERY BALL IN.

What's the point of simple, intelligent tennis if not this? To refine the sport to its essence, to improve right now and for your entire tennis career, to get closer to the inspired tennis you've envisioned for your future, you need to throw overboard the overwrought strategies, un-kink the tangle of complicated instruction and reduce the tennis ball of twine to one straight strand.

HIT EVERY BALL IN.

If you try to do it and see yourself doing it, you will improve as a player and as a competitor. You'll sharpen your concentration chops. You'll become a fakir of felt. You play tennis, now you know how to play *better* tennis. The limitless improvement you've been after comes down to one thought of unlimited usefulness and potential. The closing line please –

Go out and hit every ball in!

Ockam says.

SUPER TIE-BREAKER
(Ten Critical Points)

The ten-point super tie-breaker takes the place of a full set of tennis and can decide a match. Here are ten points that will take the place of years of on-court dues-paying and self-generated learning moments. Make your matches and hitting sessions go tour smoothly, by brushing up on (or learning for the first time) some of the courtkeeping details that round out the rough edges. So speaking of rough, here are the finer points of the outer game you can count on two, tennis-calloused hands.

1) START A RALLY

Simple start-a-rally principle number one: *hit the ball so your hitting partner can hit it back.* Drop the ball in front on you – like you're going to step into a groundstroke – and take a *medium-paced* swing through the ball, trying to land it a few feet behind your partner's service line. Despite what various friends and spouses say, success here is the uninterrupted hitting of the ball back and forth and *not* the uninterrupted running of your partner like an addled arcade duck.

2) KEEP SCORE

To double down on a friendly wager, rib a rival or appeal your latest unfairly low ranking, you need to know who won the match you just played. And have your opponent agree with you. That's where the score comes in. Fortunately, there's no need to litigate or arbitrate, the "court" with the final word here is the tennis court. Tennis scoring is based on these things: the point; the game; the set and the match. And occasionally, the line judge you requested. To win a game, win four points by a margin of two or more. To win a set, win six games by a margin of two games or more. And to win any match except a Men's Grand Slam final or a Davis Cup rubber, win two out of three sets (those others are 3 out of 5). In any game, "love" means you have no points. From there the first point is called "15", the second "30", the third "40" and the fourth, "game." The server always calls their own score first (e.g. 15–Love, 30–15, etc.) and in a game that goes to 40–40, the score is called "deuce". One player then needs to win two more points in a row to win the game. There are exceptions – the 8-game Pro Set, Super Tie-Breakers and some others – but these are the basics. On the universal scale of sports scoring difficulty, tennis is about mid-way: easier than ice-skating or cricket; harder than baseball or badminton. But hard enough to flummox the uninitiated. So before you play for pride, rankings or money, be sure to know how to score.

3) PLAY A TIE-BREAKER

Developed and refined in the 1970's, the tie-breaker and the microwave oven were both designed to fight the same problems: long waits, lack of interest and over-cooking. Forty years later, the microwave has proved easier to figure out. So here's how to play a twelve-point tie-breaker. If a set reaches 6 games all, play a tie-breaker to decide the winner. The first player to win seven points by a margin of two or more wins the set. In this quirky, hard-to-remember format, the first player serves one point from the "deuce" (right) court. After that, players alternate serving two points apiece, always starting on the "add" (left) court. Players switch ends of the court when the point total reaches six or multiples of six. By playing a tie-breaker, you add a deciding thirteenth game to a deadlocked set. Winning a tie-breaker means you win that *set* 7 – 6. Oh, and points are scored simply "0", "1", "2", "3", and so on; no 15, 30, 40, deuce. No add. No love. Weirdly or ironically, the tie-breaker started life as the VASSS, the Van Alen *Simplified* Scoring System (italics added for obvious reasons), but is now especially revered by The World Authority on Complex Kinds of Insane Tennis Tabulation, or WACKITT. And questioned by lots of players everywhere looking for scoring continuity and simplicity.

4) CALL THE LINES

When "Are you sure?" just doesn't go far enough, feel free to copy this paragraph and hand it out at your next match. The governing rules of line-calling are really simple and the intent is generous. So be generous. Basically, the benefit of the doubt in tennis always goes to the *hitter*, so a ball that is *99% out is 100% good*. (Not the other way around, as some foes would have you believe.) In fact, *99.9% out* is 100% good. In additional fact, a ball that hits the line, any part of the line or hits in such a way that you can't see space between the ball and the line is GOOD. Don't wait to see if your response shot goes in to make your call. Call your lines quickly, loudly and fair. Make sure your opponent does too. And if you have any doubt, their shot is always IN. I'm sure.

5) KNOW THE RULES

Rules rule! Get to know them better and win more matches more confidently. The rules of tennis are unique among major sports. They are few, mostly easy to remember, not typically punitive, and always favor the hitter and generally favor offense. Still, there are some nuances to know. Here's a sample hat trick of rules situations and their different outcomes. The situations:

1. You don't swing but your serve toss hits your hat.
2. Your opponent nukes a forehand that ticks your cap on its unimpeded flight to the windscreen behind you.
3. Your visor falls on the court mid-point and your opponent sees it.

The outcomes:

1. Nothing happens. It doesn't count.
2. You lose the point.
3. Play a let.

As someone once said, "There's a perfectly reasonable explanation for all of this." You'll find it in the rules.

6) MIND YOUR MANNERS

Always be polite. Always be fair. Always be honest. And act that way on the tennis court too. How exactly? Close the gate when entering or leaving a court. Wait until the point has ended or the rally has stopped to cross behind a player when walking to an adjoining court. Hit errant balls from other courts back to the server, *after* their point has stopped. Don't leave a ball on the court during a point. You or your opponent may trip over it. Pick it up or clear it to the side. Hit the ball back to your opponent *conveniently*. Hit out serves into the net, not over to the other side. Shake hands at the end of a match and thank your opponent for the match. Leave the court quickly and take your trash and leave your trash *talking* at home.

7) KEEP THE COURT ORDER

Most matches unfortunately have no line judges and no umpires; also no instant replay, no beverages or towels on tap and no trainers to call. The players are not only the contestants, they are also the ball kids, the line judges, the trainers, the coaches, the drink and towel valets and the refs. This leaves them with a big responsibility: trying to keep it all straight. And with all the stuff demanding attention in a match, it's easy to get lost trying to also remember the score. So forget the silent treatment, let you voice be heard; at least where the score is concerned. Call the score before each point, and make sure your opponent does too. That's one part of it. Make sure you start serving with two tennis balls in your possession. Clear balls that hit the net and roll onto your side of the court. Keep all the balls on the server's side of the court. In an un-officiated match with no ball kids, both players need to act like adults; even if they're juniors.

8) PICK UP A BALL

A whole section on this? How hard can it be? Bend over and pick it up. Yes, and if engineers designed buildings, they'd all be boxes. And yet there are architects. Be the architect of your own court cool: learn some cool-player ball pick-ups: bounce the ball up with the strings; hold it next to your shoe and cradle it up, or better yet, scoop the ball off the court with your racquet barely touching the surface. Make it elegant and aesthetic. Look like someone who's played. Even if it's your second week, other players will think it's been a month or more.

9) CATCH A BALL ON THE RACQUET

All strokes and no sizzle make for a dull player. In the realm of cool on the court, this one is subtle, deft and quietly flashy. You can catch a ball on your stringbed like the pros and the teaching pros by following these simple tips: keep your hands light on the grip; match the speed of your catching racquet to the ball speed and curl the racquet head under the ball. If the racquet is held too firmly, the ball bounces off the strings. If you don't watch the ball closely, you may end up trying to catch with the frame. It takes practice to master this bit of racquet-digitation, but as court tricks go it's one of the best; easier than hitting the ball behind the back and safer than hitting between the legs.

10) DRESS FOR THE GAME

Wear tennis clothes. Wear tennis shoes. Look good winning or losing. Hold your head high, stick to your game and remember to bring two new cans of tennis balls and cold water for both of you.

Play on!

APPENDIX A
FAQ:TS

(Frequently Answered Questions: Tennis Specific)

"If you don't ask, you don't get."

Mahatma Gandhi

I've been asked quite a few questions over the years. (Many of them even related to tennis). This is a partial list of the some of the most-asked tennis questions on the teaching court.

Q – How old is the game of tennis?

A – Very old. Even older than snowboarding. It goes back to Egypt and Persia. Lawn tennis officially began in England in 1873 thanks to the annuity and ingenuity of Walter Wingfield, a retired army major with free time, social connections and a love of sports. He based his game, "sphairistike" on Jeu de Paume (the game of the palm), a recreation popular with monks in 13th century France. In that version it was played with the *hand* hitting the ball. Racquets weren't involved until about three centuries later; *really good* racquets, not until the 1970's.

Late in the 19th century, the game migrated to America. As with golf, the modern game began to take shape around 1870 with the discovery of vulcanized rubber, which produced the modern tennis ball. With the invent of Open Tennis in 1968, professional tennis went legit; managers, agents, endorsements, fan sites, big money, bigger egos and celebrity marriages followed.

Q – Where does the word "tennis" come from?

A – From Old French, "tenez", to take or receive; announced by server to opponent. Strong historical proof that the serve is the backbone of the game. Even so, the 16th century royals had servants put the ball in play for them. To which I humbly suggest, bring back this method and watch tennis participation soar, and student frustration plummet.

Q – What about the word "love'?

A – A very nice word that in tennis means nothing. Literally. Opinions of its origins vary. It's either from "love of the game"; that is, not for the money (probably an outdated usage), or from the French word "l'oeuff", the egg, because of the resemblance of an egg to a zero. At least for the 21st century pro, the latter seems likelier.

Q – How big is a tennis court?

A – Depends on the day. Some days it's a football field, other days a ping-pong table. Actual dimensions: 36 x 78 feet.

Q – How high is the net?

A – Depends on the shot. Depends on the opponent. Depends on the day. Actual dimensions: 36 inches on center and 42 inches above the sidelines. The high percentage play is crosscourt; low net (36") and long court (85'). The risky, heroic low percentage play is down-the-line; high net (42") and shorter (78') court. So do the math and choose your path.

Q – Is the court the pros play on the same size as the one we play on?

A – Yes, but television adds 15 pounds. So does the perfectly legal expansion of the area behind the baseline and outside the sidelines. (Think: Arthur Ashe Stadium at the US Open.)

Q – Why does tennis have such a weird scoring system?

A – It's an old sport. People were weird back then. But blame the French if you must. In the sports' ancient and regal scoring system, a "game" equals one hour on a clock face. The first point of the game is called 15 (a quarter past the hour), the second 30 (half-past the hour), the third, 40 (originally 45; three quarters past) and "game" being a return to the top of the hour. It's not the least apt metaphor. Some deuce games seems like they really take that long.

Q – What are the four majors of modern tennis?

A – A clothing/shoe contract, a racquet contract, an airline endorsement and a watch deal. Or more conventionally, the Australian Open (January/February), Roland Garros (the French Open) (May/June), Wimbledon (June/July) and the US OPEN (August/September).

Q – What is winning a "major", exactly?

A – Two definitions: 1) Being champion at any one of the four major tournaments, and 2) An endorsement that exceeds your yearly prize money.

Q – What is *A* Grand Slam and what is *The* Grand Slam?

A – *A* Grand Slam is the same as a Major. *The* Grand Slam is winning all four Majors in a calendar year **or** getting all four endorsements before you've won a Major.

Q – What is a "Career Slam"?

A – Two definitions: 1) Winning all four Majors in your career; 2) An endorsement deal that outlives your career. Both nifty feats.

Q – What is the "Golden Slam"?

A – All four Majors and an Olympic Gold. Or, all four endorsements *and* a celebrity fiance. Even niftier.

Q – How many court surfaces are there?

A – Basically three: Hardcourt (US Open and Australian Open), Clay (Roland Garros) and Grass (Wimbledon). Hardcourts are typically made of asphalt on top of concrete, though both the US and Australian Opens are played on synthetic ashphalt. Clay is made from crushed stone or brick in the case of Roland Garros. And the grass court at Wimbledon is very much like a putting green.

Q – Why are there three different court surfaces?

A – So that a bunch of players no one in the U.S. has ever heard of dominate the tour every Spring.

APPENDIX A

Q – What's so different about the "Modern Power Game"?

A – It's modern. And it's more powerful. Some strokes – extreme topspin forehands, open-stance backhands, swinging volleys – have changed both the speed of the shot and the ability of players to create offense from more areas of the court. Increased prize money has attracted better athletes with bigger retinues who are better conditioned and hit the ball with an abundance of power and an injury-inducing lack of sound technique. But it's okay, they can afford lots of physical therapy and early retirements.

Q – Tennis announcers credit modern racquets and strings for the drastic increase in power. Is this true?

A – Partially; although, very few announcers have ever worked in tennis retail, or spent time with equipment reps at trade shows and demo days. (Their loss, clearly.) Like most teaching pros, most announcers only know about the racquet they play with and know even less about strings they or anybody else plays with. They do know how to say "advantage Schmmimildoober", "hit the ball through the court" and "this is a big point", though.

The facts are these. The racquets that many of the very powerful pros play with have basically the same amount of power as the racquet that Pete Sampras started with over twenty years ago. In size, weight and thickness they are also basically the same. And though there are larger, thicker and stiffer racquets made, the pros do not tend to use the most powerful ones. As with golf, power is not difficult for the pros to achieve. Acquiring better control and feel are what help them win. Those two things will also help *you* win.

Q – Very few of the pros seem to serve and volley anymore. Is it worth it for me to try this strategy?

A – Yes. Ignore what the pros do. Because of the very well-conditioned opponents on the pro tour, it is difficult for a serve-and-volley player to respond to the increased speed of returns and passing shots. In such an environment, serve and volley tennis is a low percentage gamble. And the pro tour is a lot like a high school. No one wants to be different. Could be because most of the players are high school age and most of the coaches want to be.

Serve-and-volley is a useful tactic in the recreational game: if only for a change of pace. The sight of the other player advancing to the net can be psychologically devastating to an opponent. And against strokes that don't move at pro speed, the odds of getting passed are much slimmer. As has been pointed out by other writers, it is possible to create more devastating angles from the net than from the backcourt and therefore coming in to the net can be a major offensive advantage. Plus it looks very athletic and gives your hair that windblown look.

Q – How often should I re-string?

A – Whenever your strings break.

Q – Or?

A – Or as many times per year as you play per week. Minimum, once a year.

Q – Thanks.

A – Was that a question?

Q – Was that an answer?

A – And on we go.

Q – How often should I re-grip? (Okay. I put this question in here. I'm never asked this, though I should be.)

A – *Every 20 hours of play.* And if it's a white or light-colored grip, it's easier to know when. (Hint: The grip will look dingy, dirty and disgusting.) (Second Hint: It's *not* supposed to look that way.)

Q – How often should I get a new racquet?

A – Every 200 Hours of play or when your local retailer needs a little revenue pick-me-up. **Or** when *you* need a little pick-me-up. **Or** when the racquet cracks or breaks.

Q – Should I wear tennis shoes?

A – Who asked that? It's *tennis*, isn't it?

Q – What about running shoes?

A –Excellent for running. (By the way, who asked *that?*) Running is a part of most tennis training regimens. However, running shoes are made to travel forward, not sideways. Tennis shoes are made to support your feet and ankles in all directions of movement. They also resist abrasion from the court much better and their grippy soles remind you to stop before you hit.

Q – How often should I buy new shoes?

A – When they *don't* remind you to stop before you hit. Or, when they have worn soles, stop cushioning your feet, have holes in the soles or a new style comes out that you just *have* to have.

Q – How often should I change tennis balls?

A – Every time you play.

Q – Really?

A – Really. Cross my court and hope for a bye.

Q – Why doesn't the ball bounce as high on a cold day?

A – Gay-Lussac's Law. My only positive takeaway, and in fact my *only* takeaway from high school chemistry. This law says that when the temperature drops in a closed system like a tennis ball, so does the pressure in that system. The internal pressure is what gives the ball its bounce. The good news is you can swing away more on a cold day. By the way, hot days make the ball bounce higher. But you probably guessed that.

Q – I'm a woman tennis player. Is there anything particular tennis will do for me?

A – Besides being great aerobic and anaerobic exercise, outdoor tennis will aid in vitamin D intake and most importantly, since tennis is an impact exercise, this will increase bone density and helps prevent Osteoporosis. Who would've guessed that asphalt and concrete would promote healthy living?

APPENDIX A

Q – I've never been very athletic. Will I be able to play?

A – Yes, trust me on this one. Here's why. Tennis is much more about good stroke mechanics and early movement to the ball than about blinding speed, superior strength or extraordinary vertical leap. And if you've ever seen me play, you'd know you can believe me.

Q – Will I ever be able to stop *thinking* about my strokes, and just flow?

A – Hard to say for sure. Sometimes, yes; always, probably not. Tennis strokes are sensitive enough that even very experienced players return again and again to review their basics in order to correct or keep strokes on track. In the teaching pro circles, this is called "Job Security".

Q – How much should I practice?

A – As much as you can. One lesson a week will improve you. Add a hitting session and you'll improve more. Add another and you're cooking. Add more than that and you're self-employed, unemployed or trust-funded. Keep your job, but the more practice the better.

Q – How much do the pros practice?

A – Every day. Or more often if they can.

Q – Is it possible to practice *too much*?

A – Sure. After a tough tournament or season, or an injury, reduce your practice time so you can rest and recover to come back even stronger.

Also reduce your practice if you want to give your opponents time to catch up with you.

Q – Why do my strokes feel weird after a layoff?

A – Because they're mad at you for abandoning them. And since tennis is so much about fine adjustments to ball bounce height, foot position and swing angle, these adjustments go off quickly when a stroke is out of practice.

Q – Who is the best tennis player ever?

A – The one that you like the best. Equipment, fitness, tournament fields and tournament venues vary so tremendously that it is next to impossible to compare various eras and player's records. And that is my final, official, non-controversial, non-confrontational true but bland answer. In other words, by all means check the stats, but it's personal preference.

Q – How can I be a great tennis player?

A – Winning 25 Grand Slams, an Olympic gold and the Fed or Davis cup is of course one way. Or as with so many other pursuits, decide how much you want to dedicate yourself to the game and try to follow your own path to whatever level of proficiency means excellence to you – whether in rallies or in games.

Beyond that, savor every moment of every day and if possible make tennis a part of your daily enjoyment. Remember, that even on an difficult day playing tennis, you are still outside participating in an enjoyable, healthy, life-affirming activity.

APPENDIX A

Q – At what age should my child start playing?

A – Why wait? Turn Tennis Channel on when the child is in the womb. Start the indoctrination early. If there's still interest *after birth*, a child can start as soon as he or she can swing a small racquet and stand up. Hang a Nerf ball at their waist height in the garage and let him or her hit it and hit at it. Start lessons when they're ready and stop lessons if they're tired or their attention is wandering. Make it fun and they'll keep coming back to it. Make it a dirge and they'll turn pro and out you as an abuser later in their tell-all bio and lecture tour.

Q – My son / daughter wants to be a pro. What should I do?

A – Quit your job. Sell the house. Drain the savings and the IRA and move immediately to Bradenton and sign up at the Academy. Then sit back and watch the little money machine work hard to bank your retirement. Or –

Read to them. Talk to them. Make sure they get a good education. Love them unconditionally. Support their desire to pursue their dreams, while remembering to create balance in their lives. Support them if they want to take lessons and play tournaments. Make sure at each step that the dreams being pursued are *their* dreams, not *your* dreams.

If, after finishing high school, your child wants to go pro and has a chance of making it, consider having them defer college and try it, remembering all the while that only an infinitesimally small percentage of players end up as playing pros each decade.

However, know that there are other career opportunities in tennis. If your child really loves the game, perhaps he or she can find a way to stay in the game by teaching it, running tournaments, being a sales rep for a tennis product line, being an agent or trainer or marketing person. Or, if all else fails, writing a tennis book.

Q – More questions? Better answers? Please e-mail me at: marcuscootsona.com.

APPENDIX B
SHORT ON IDEAS

(The Simple Six)

SIX SIMPLE WAYS TO IMPROVE YOUR TENNIS *TODAY*

1. STROKE *SLOWER*.

2. STOP BEFORE YOU HIT.

3. DON'T HIT AN UN-HITTABLE TOSS.

4. GET A RESTRING.

5. FINISH ALL OF YOUR STROKES.

6. BREATHE.

AND –

6A. READ THIS BOOK AGAIN.

APPENDIX C
MAKIN' A LIST

(The Rankings)

Tennis loves rankings. Ranking the players. Ranking their strokes. Ranking their statistics. Some individuals with advanced math degrees and a lot of free time even follow them. Some of *them* understand them. I'm not in either camp. So I thought I'd come up with my own rankings. Here in short order, are the strokes to be learned –

THE PRIMARY GAME

1. Forehand Groundstroke

2. Backhand Groundstroke

3. Serve.

4. Forehand Volley

5. Backhand Volley

6. Overhead

7. Forehand Half-volley

8. Backhand Half-volley

9. Backhand Overhead

THE SECONDARY GAME

1. Topspin Forehand

2. Slice Backhand

3. Slice and Kick Serve

4. Drop Shot

5. Slice Forehand

6. Topspin Backhand

ABOUT THE AUTHOR

Marcus Cootsona is an award-winning tennis retailer and lapsed playwright who instructs tennis students one at a time in Atherton, California. He lives with his wife, son and two dogs he is teaching to play.

Made in the USA
Lexington, KY
09 January 2014